HOLISTIC FIRST AID

HOLISTIC FIRST AID

A HANDBOOK FOR THE HOME

DR MICHAEL NIGHTINGALE

An OPTIMA book

First published in 1988 by
Macdonald Optima, a division of
Macdonald & Co. (Publishers) Ltd

A Pergamon Press PLC company

British Library Cataloguing in Publication Data

Nightingale, Michael
  Holistic first aid.
  1. Man. Health. Holism — Manuals
  I. Title
  613
    ISBN 0-356-15198-0

Macdonald & Co. (Publishers) Ltd
3rd Floor
Greater London House
Hampstead Road
London NW1 7QX

Illustrations by the Maltings Partnership, Derby

Edited with additional material by Fiona Lawson

Typeset by Leaper & Gard Ltd, Bristol, England
Printed and bound in Great Britain by
The Guernsey Press Co. Ltd
Guernsey, Channel Islands

CONTENTS

HOW TO USE THIS BOOK   6

INTRODUCTION   7

THE THERAPIES   10
  Homeopathy   10
  The Bach Flower remedies   14
  Acupuncture and Chinese medicine   17
  Osteopathy   23
  Hydrotherapy   25

A-Z OF COMMON AILMENTS   27

FIRST AID   148

REFERENCE   165
  Using acupressure   165
  Yoga postures   178
  Vitamins and minerals   182
  Liver drainage   186
  Elimination diet   187
  Useful addresses   188
  A holistic First Aid box   191

ABOUT THE AUTHOR   192

HOW TO USE THIS BOOK

Following a short introduction, the book is divided into four main parts:

1   THE THERAPIES (pages 10-26)
This gives general information about the different therapies referred to in the text, and the principles on which they operate.

2   A-Z OF COMMON AILMENTS (pages 27-147)
Here you can look up recommendations for treating a wide range of complaints. In most cases, more than one sort of treatment has been suggested. Try to put as many as possible into practice, but do not worry if you cannot manage them all.

For the homeopathic remedies, try to match your particular symptoms to the descriptions given — they indicate which remedy would suit you best.

3   FIRST AID (pages 148-164)
This describes the treatment to be applied in emergency situations. Again it is arranged alphabetically. Combining traditional First Aid with holistic remedies will optimize the body's chance of recovery.

4   REFERENCE (pages 165-191)
This includes details of techniques such as acupressure and yoga which are referred to in the text, with full instructions on how to apply them (with illustrations), plus nutritional information, useful addresses, and advice on preparing a holistic First Aid box.

INTRODUCTION

Most of us are born healthy, and many of us assume that ill-health befalls us through no fault of our own. Disease is nearly always seen as an unfortunate accident.

Most modern medical theories would seem to support this notion. Disease and ill-health are described as the results of congenital defects, infections such as bacteria or viruses, accidents or just bad luck. Even those illnesses which can be clearly related to self-inflicted causes, such as lung cancer in heavy smokers or cirrhosis of the liver in heavy drinkers, are still often attributed to unlucky chance rather than stupidity. At the same time, having someone ask for a carrot juice instead of a beer is still seen as a way of raising a laugh on television 'comedy' programmes.

Almost at the opposite extreme is the theory which suggests that we develop diseases for psychological reasons. Every physician knows that there are some people who cannot let go of their illness because it is the only thing that brings them the attention they crave. However, it seems unlikely that, for example, many smokers really want to die, slowly and painfully, from a disease as debilitating and prolonged as lung cancer.

Why, then, do so many people develop unhealthy habits? Why do so many people ignore the laws of nature and push themselves into ill-health? Some 2,000 years ago the famous Chinese Yellow Emperor blamed his people's reduced lifespan on 'reckless behaviour, over-indulgence in alcohol, giving in to cravings, not being content with themselves'. How much — or how little — has changed since then?

Times *are* changing. Many people are eating less meat — or no meat at all — and more fibre, taking more exercise and cutting down on smoking and drinking. Many items on the supermarket shelves proudly display stickers stating 'No artificial ingredients' — even if they still contain high quantities of 'natural' white sugar, salt and refined flour!

And gradually, more and more people are coming to accept that — while illness is obviously best prevented altogether — so long as it exists, it is better to treat the whole person rather than the symptoms alone. Such a holistic approach does not merely treat the whole person, but is concerned with the balance of body, mind and spirit, and seeks to promote the vital, innate healing force that is in us all. It sees good health as the result of living in conformity with certain natural laws, and disease as the body's attempt to return to balance or harmony. Holistic medicine employs health-promoting methods to help the body to achieve this objective. (The suppression of symptoms, so often the effect of modern drugs, merely stifles the body's attempt at true healing and drives the problem deeper.)

This book on holistic First Aid and simple treatments offers the first line of approach. Most of the standard First Aid measures for emergencies, which can be found in any conventional First Aid manual, are entirely in line with it. For example, the restoration of breathing, the arrest of bleeding, restarting a heart that has stopped beating and dealing with shock are all commonsense matters, and cannot be described as either drug-based or holistic in approach. However, the administration of homeopathic arnica montana for bruising and shock, aconititum napellus for fright and hypericum for pain and nerve damage (all of which are completely neglected in the standard works), would dramatically improve the patient's condition, reduce the time spent in hospital and thus save much needed money. They frequently produce such benefits as less scarring, less trauma to the system and more complete healing; and in some cases hospitalization could be avoided altogether.

Armed with basic knowledge it is possible to help in emergencies such as road traffic accidents, drowning or acute poisoning, but the majority of problems discussed here are the day-to-day ills which beset the average person or family. The simple procedures suggested use common sense, homeopathic remedies, massage of acupuncture or reflex points and the administration of herbs, spices or natural substances such as ice, essential oils, vitamins or other nutrients.

Sometimes, more professional help is recommended, and outlines of the main holistic therapies are given in the following section. Nutritional advice is also included and at the end of the book you will find a list of useful addresses to help you find a suitable practitioner. The choice of whom to see — orthodox medical doctor or 'alternative' practitioner — is yours. In some cases — for example, broken bones — treatment by orthodox means is inevitable and indeed recommended, but even then holistic treatment can often go hand-in-hand with traditional.

Modern drugs are very often harmful in some way; and when drug-based treatment is unavoidable it is at least sensible to couple it with holistic therapies to help counteract the damage. For example, antibiotics should always be taken with additional vitamin B complex and vitamin C, and the course should be followed by homeopathic nux vomica and recolonization of the gut with acidophilus baccili, as antibiotics destroy the beneficial bacteria which occur naturally in the gut. If you consider that 10 per cent of hospital patients catch a disease while there, and that 40 per cent of patients taking drugs experience side effects often more serious than the condition for which they are being treated, the hidden dangers of conventional medicine can be seen.

The purpose of this book is not merely to provide simple remedies with which you can obtain relief from numerous complaints, but also to introduce the concept that holistic treatment implies a regeneration of the whole person. The treatment is not concerned with the suppression or mere removal of symptoms, but the rooting out of the basic cause of the problem. In fact we can go deeper than the physical body and ask some pertinent questions. Why do these symptoms occur? Are they trying to teach us something? Are there lessons to be learned? Only by looking to see where we are going wrong and correcting the errors can we hope to make any kind of real improvement. If the medical treatment we are following fails to help us improve our long-term health, it is neither holistic nor, in the last analysis, useful.

In the A-Z section (p. 27 onwards), a number of different forms of treatment have been suggested for each ailment. These should not be seen as conflicting; most of them can be combined without difficulty. Some of the treatments are important for everyone; others may be selected as required. In all cases, the aim is to promote the healing process and to assist the body to heal itself.

Finally, remember that adequate relaxation is vital for good health. There seems little point in working so hard that you have no time to relax, and then to die before you can enjoy the fruits of the labour that killed you! 'Enjoy life' is probably the greatest of all axioms. Perhaps the next is that 'laughter is the best medicine'. I hope this book will encourage you along the path to a healthy, fulfilled and happy life.

THE THERAPIES

HOMEOPATHY

THE DISCOVERY OF HOMEOPATHY

Homeopathy means 'treating like with like'. It was formulated in its classic form by a Prussian doctor, Christian Samuel Hahnemann, who was born in Meissen (now in East Germany) in 1755. He studied medicine at Leipzig University and worked as a doctor for a number of years before becoming disillusioned with medicine as it was practised at the time.

It was in 1790 that Hahnemann was led to the formulation of homeopathy. He could not accept the explanation given for the way in which drugs worked and decided that the only way to discover their true action was to test them on himself. He started with cinchona, and found to his surprise that when he took this drug it produced in him the very symptoms of the diseases which it was being used to cure: namely intermittent fever or ague. He experimented in the same way with a large number of other drugs and also persuaded his friends to be 'guinea pigs' for him. These test were termed 'the provings' and eventually resulted in the Law of Similars, upon which a new branch of medicine would come to be constructed.

THE LAW OF SIMILARS

Hahnemann was now able to predict the action of every drug then known, and he propounded a system of medicine in which the symptoms of the patient were matched to the 'symptoms' of the drug. Although this idea was not new — it had even been known in Hippocrates's time — it took the genius of Hahnemann to incorporate it into a complete system of medicine. This principle is known as The Law of Similars and is the foundation of homeopathy.

THE MINIMUM DOSE

In trying to find the smallest amount of a drug that would still work, Hahnemann was surprised to find that the drugs were still effective when diluted and given in tiny doses. This principle, which he incorporated into homeopathy, is known as the Law of the Minimum Dose.

MIASMS

According to Hahnemann all acute diseases, if suppressed, would be driven deeper into the body and would then be passed on through the next generation as 'taints' of disease. These became known as miasms.

POLYCRESTS

These are the homeopathic drugs which have the commonest symptoms in their provings and, consequently, they are the most frequently used remedies. Because of their ability to reproduce common symptoms, they often act as anti-miasmic remedies.

SUCCUSSION AND POTENCY

Hahnemann later discovered that by shaking the remedies vigorously (a process which came to be known as *succussion*), they became much more potent. What was potentised was not the substance itself, Hahnemann believed, but a force, a vibration which was imparted to the solution and acted on the subtle levels of the body to encourage the natural healing process.

When a drug was diluted one part in ten and succussed, it was termed a 1× potency. In Europe this is often expressed as 1D. When a drop of the 1× is added to nine drops of solution and succussed again, it becomes a 2× and so on. The most commonly used potency nowadays in this range is 6×, but sometimes a 12× is used. Another type of dilution, known as the centesimal dilution, is when the drug is diluted one part in a hundred. The first dilution is 1c. The lowest potency commonly used in this range is a 30c (or simply '30') which means that the drug has been diluted this way thirty times over. A 200 means that the drug has been diluted, at the rate of one part in a hundred, two hundred times over.

THE BASIS OF PRESCRIPTION

Homeopaths treat an individual who has a disease, rather than the disease itself. This is why a thorough understanding of the patient is very important. A good homeopath will not only want to know what the symptoms are: he or she will also wish to know how you feel at different times of the day, if you are tidy or untidy, if you weep easily or not, how you are affected by the weather, if you like being alone or always need company, whether you like hot or cold drinks, whether you sip or gulp your drinks, and more. He or she will also ask a wide variety of questions about the pain or symptoms you are experiencing.

COMPLEX HOMEOPATHY

Although Hahnemann himself used only one remedy at a time, many modern practitioners use mixtures of low potency homeopathic remedies. These are carefully designed to deal with each aspect of a disease. For example, a complex remedy for fever will contain one remedy for fever, another for congestion in the head, another to stimulate the immune system, another to increase sweating, another to increase kidney activity and improve elimination and another to regulate the temperature.

TISSUE SALTS

Human tissue is made up of a number of salts. Another homeopath, Dr Wilhelm Schuessler, claimed that disease often resulted from a deficiency (or occasionally, an excess) of one or more of these salts. He believed that other remedies worked because of their content of these salts and that taking the correct salt, in homeopathic potency, would then give a 'message' to the body to start absorbing more of that salt naturally (or less, in cases where there was already an excess). The table opposite gives the names of the main salts and their chief effects on the body.

HOW TO TAKE HOMEOPATHIC REMEDIES

It is important to follow certain rules when taking homeopathic remedies as they are quite unlike ordinary medicines.

Take the remedy at least half an hour before a meal, *or* two hours after a meal. If the remedy is taken within two hours of eating, it may not work properly. The best time to take them is last thing at night and first thing in the morning.

Do not touch the remedies. Shake the required dose into the lid of the container and tip it into the mouth. Do not allow the container lid to touch the mouth. Under no circumstances replace a pill into the container if it has been handled.

If the medicine is in liquid form, there will usually be a dropper or dispenser included. In this case shake the required number of drops into the mouth without allowing the dropper to touch the lips.

Do not drink coffee or eat or drink peppermint whilst taking the homeopathic remedy as these affect the action of the remedy.

Keep the tablets or drops in the mouth for a minute or two before attempting to swallow them.

Do not clean your teeth with toothpaste for at least half an hour and preferably two hours after taking the remedy.

Be careful not to store the medicine where there is any strong scent, especially camphor or eucalyptus.

Do not take a very hot bath after taking a remedy.

TISSUE SALTS		
Common name	**Latin name**	**Effect**
SODIUM PHOSPHATE	NATRUM PHOSPHORICUM	Neutralises lactic acids, prevents cholesterol crystals forming
SODIUM SULPHATE	NATRUM SULPHURICUM	Stimulates bile and balances level of water in body
SODIUM CHLORIDE	NATRUM MURIATICUM	Regulates distribution of water and red blood cells
POTASSIUM CHLORIDE	KALIUM MURIATICUM	Stimulates cell activity and helps with inflammation
POTASSIUM PHOSPHATE	KALIUM PHOSPHORICUM	Aids nervous system and tones muscles and prevents degeneration
POTASSIUM SULPHATE	KALIUM SULPHURICUM	Oxygenates cells and maintains healthy skin and nails
MAGNESIUM PHOSPHATE	MAGNESIA PHOSPHORICA	Enables cells to eliminate waste and relaxes muscles
SILICONE DIOXIDE	SILICA	Firms tissue, eliminates pus
CALCIUM PHOSPHATE	CALCAREA PHOSPHORICA	Improves health of bones; prevents haemorrhaging
CALCIUM FLUORIDE	CALCAREA FLUORICA	Strengthens tissue
IRON PHOSPHATE	FERRUM PHOSPHORICUM	Oxygenates blood and copes with inflammation

DOSAGE

Unless you know what you are doing or the treatment has been prescribed by a homeopath, do not take remedies of a higher potency than 30.

In general, acute problems are treated by doses of low potency taken frequently; while chronic problems require high potency doses taken only once or twice a day.

FIRST AID USES OF HOMEOPATHY

You may wonder how it is possible to use homeopathic, remedies for First Aid purposes when one has to know so much about the patient to prescribe them. In fact, the answer is quite simple. In First Aid, we are treating only a specific symptom that has been imposed upon the person accidentally. When you cut yourself, it does not matter whether you are fair or dark, fat or thin, happy or depressed. All that matters is that you have a cut and that the remedies calendula and hypericum will help the body to heal the cut, whoever you are and whatever your state of health.

In the First Aid section, suggested potencies for the homeopathic remedies have not been given, as this is generally unimportant in emergencies. Either 6× or 30c may be given, according to what is available. The 6× should be given more frequently.

THE BACH FLOWER REMEDIES

The Bach Flower remedies are similar to homeopathic preparations in that they are very dilute, do not work on a purely physical basis and are prescribed on indications of the patient's character and emotional state rather than on physical symptoms.

Edward Bach was a Welshman who qualified as a doctor at University College, London and subsequently gained his diploma in Public Health at Cambridge in 1913. Even as a student he was more interested in patients as people than in their diseases. He noted that certain patients recovered more quickly than others and that these people were invariably the ones who were happy, emotionally healthy and positive in their thinking. He noted that those who were full of negative emotions, such as anxiety and worry, recovered much more slowly and he came to the conclusion that the body merely reflected the prevailing mental or emotional condition. He decided that the real basis of disease was in the mind or spirit, and that such patients needed help to overcome any negative thinking before they could recover properly. He began to prescribe exclusively according to the patient's temperament, and was extremely successful. In 1930, at the peak of his career, Dr Bach abandoned his medical practice in order to pursue a strong inner conviction that the solution to human ills could be found in the wild plants and trees of the countryside. Over the following seven years he assiduously searched for the plants which would provide him with the confirmation of his theories. He became extremely sensitive and was able to experiment on himself with different plant qualities as he discovered them.

Dr Bach eventually discovered thirty-eight different wild plants, all completely harmless, which he believed would heal the unhappy mental states which predisposed certain people to disease and impaired their recovery. He prepared the flowers by picking them early in the morning and placing them in a glass bowl with water, then exposing the bowl to sunlight for a few hours. The water would become activated with tiny bubbles. He then decanted the water, bottled and preserved it with a little brandy. In the case of early blossoms e.g. from trees, Dr Bach covered them with water in a sterile container, boiled them gently for half an hour and removed the flowers after cooling. The liquid would then be filtered and bottled with a little brandy as before. This is how the remedies are still prepared today, under strict supervision.

THE THIRTY-EIGHT FLOWER REMEDIES
These can be classified into seven groups, according to the predominant emotion.

FEAR	
Aspen:	Vague fears that something terrible will happen.
Cherry plum:	Fear of doing something impulsive and immoral.
Mimulus:	Fear of specific things, e.g. accidents, poverty, speaking in public.
Rock rose:	Terror (often used after accidents).
Star of Bethlehem:	For shock from bad news.
DESPONDENCY	
Crab apple:	Feels unclean, ashamed of self. Often houseproud.
Elm:	Temporary feelings of inadequacy and inability to cope with responsibilities.
Larch:	Expects failure, lacks confidence.
Oak:	Brave, determined type that 'plods on'.
Pine:	Lacks self-respect. Has guilt complex.
Sweet chestnut:	Extreme anguish — reached limit of endurance.

UNCERTAINTY

Cerato:	Those who doubt their own judgement.
Gentian:	Easily discouraged, has negative outlook on life.
Gorse:	Feeling of hopelessness and despair.
Hornbeam:	Procrastinates. Can't get going.
Scleranthus:	Indecision. Fluctuating moods.
Wild oat:	Helps to determine one's intended path in life.

LACK OF INTEREST

Chestnut bud:	Does not learn by experience.
Clematis:	Preoccupied, absent-minded and dreamy.
Honeysuckle:	Nostalgia, often homesick, longs for the past.
Mustard:	Sudden 'dark cloud' descends for no apparent reason.
Olive:	Drained of energy: everything is an effort.
White chestnut:	Persistent unwanted thoughts and mental arguments.
Wild rose:	Drifts, without ambition. Apathetic.

LONELINESS

Heather:	Talkative, self-centred bore.
Impatiens:	Impatient and irritable.
Water violet:	Proud, reserved, sometimes superior.

OVER-SENSITIVITY TO INFLUENCE AND IDEAS

Willow:	Resentment and bitterness.
Agrimony:	Inner torture with facade of cheerfulness.
Centaury:	Can't say no. 'Human doormat' type.
Holly:	Jealous, vengeful, envious and suspicious.
Walnut:	Helps adjust to change e.g. puberty, menopause or against adverse outside influences.

EXCESSIVE CARE FOR WELFARE OF OTHERS

Beech:	Arrogant and critical of others.
Chicory:	Over-possessive, expects everyone else to conform to his/her own standards.
Rock water:	Rigid in outlook, very hard on self.
Vervain:	Fanatic, incensed by injustice. Forces self beyond capabilities.
Vine:	Dominating, inflexible and ambitious.
Red chestnut:	Anxiety and fear for other people.

The remedies have to be taken regularly for a period of several weeks at least, as they can work quite slowly. Nevertheless, they often have a dramatic influence, improving attitude as well as helping with recovery from illness.

THE RESCUE REMEDY
Dr Bach also combined five remedies to formulate an emergency remedy for situations such as shock, receipt of bad news, accidents, interviews and exams. The Rescue Remedy combines cherry plum, clematis, impatiens, rock rose and star of Bethlehem. It is available as a liquid remedy, but also as a cream for application to bites, stings, burns etc.

HOW TO TAKE THE REMEDIES
Unlike homeopathic medicines, Bach remedies may be taken on a regular basis and with food. Usually a few drops of the remedy is put in a glass of water and sipped slowly, but they can be taken direct from the bottle with the dropper and held in the mouth for a moment before swallowing.

The remedies are available from many health food shops and herbalists, as well as direct from the Bach Flower centre (see p. 188). It is advisable to consult a naturopath for an initial diagnosis and prescription — but if treating yourself, try to be very honest about your own character when choosing remedies.

ACUPUNCTURE AND CHINESE MEDICINE

Acupuncture is a system of medicine in which fine needles are placed in certain points of the body to help relieve stagnation of blood and energy. It formed part of the ancient Chinese school of medicine which incorporated herbal medicine, heat treatment, massage and manipulation, and relaxation therapy. Acupuncture was practised many thousands of years ago in China, and also in many other parts of the East. It is still widely practised in many countries today.

The points in which the needles are placed are often known as acupoints and are distributed all over the body, linked by channels known as meridians. The meridians all relate to specific organs of the body (e.g. the liver) or functions (e.g. the purification of the blood). Energy (known as *Chi*) flows along the meridians and by placing needles in particular meridians, acupuncturists claim to be able to heal the organ to which the meridian is linked, even if the acupoint is nowhere near the organ, by clearing the energy (Chi) which flows along the meridian line.

YIN AND YANG

According to ancient theory, the body can only be healthy when everything — Chi energy, blood and fluids, including the hormones and the nervous system — are in harmony. In terms of the ancient Chinese philosophy, this balance is expressed in terms of yin and yang. The ancient Chinese depicted yin as the dark side of the hill, with the properties of coldness, dampness and darkness, while yang represents the sunny side, which is light, dry and hot. Everything in the universe, it was believed, was made up of its rightful proportion of yin and yang. The human being is unique in standing between heaven and earth: attracting the yang force of heaven (the sun) and the yin force of the earth. If the balance of yin and yang is upset, illness occurs. The Chinese physician looks far deeper than the physical symptoms, because it is believed that the vital principle of balanced energy is vastly more important than the material body.

CHI: THE VITAL FORCE

According to the Chinese, the energy or Chi was the 'blueprint' of the physical body, and their attention was therefore concentrated on the study of Chi rather than on the physical body itself. Consequently, their view of anatomy and physiology differed from our modern Western concepts.

It is interesting that, although they seldom looked at dead bodies, the ancient Chinese understood much more about the body than their contemporaries elsewhere. They anticipated Harvey's discovery of the circulation of the blood by nearly two thousand years!

ACUPUNCTURE TODAY

Many physicians today use what they consider to be the best methods from both worlds: the ancient Chinese deductive, vitalistic system and the modern scientific, analytical approach. Careful synthesis of the two can provide excellent results, and modern methods of stimulating the acupoints such as laser therapy and electromagnetism amply compensate for our present-day problems of lack of time and more complicated illnesses.

CONDITIONS BEST TREATED BY ACUPUNCTURE

The conditions which respond best to acupuncture treatment are functional disorders such as headache, migraine, sinusitis, neuralgia, asthma, many kinds of back pain, sciatica, tiredness, muscular aches and pains, some skin problems, diarrhoea, constipation and stomach disorders.

Acupuncture has to be carried out by a trained practitioner

and is not a therapy that can be practised at home. However, massaging the acupoints with a fingertip, thumb or knuckle is an extremely effective home remedy for many ailments. Sometimes a blunt instrument, such as the bottom or cap of a ball-point pen, needs to be used on very small areas such as the base of a fingernail. (See recommendations in the A-Z section and instructions on Using Acupressure, pp. 165-177.)

ACUPRESSURE

Acupressure is a very similar treatment to acupuncture, using gentle pressure of the hands on certain parts of the body, rather than needles. It should be carried out by a trained practitioner as it is a very precise treatment, used when areas of the body are

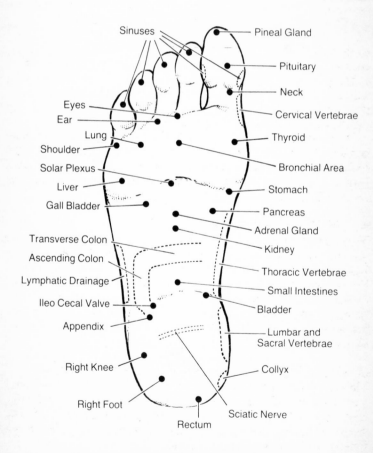

Sinuses
Pineal Gland
Pituitary
Neck
Eyes
Ear
Cervical Vertebrae
Lung
Thyroid
Shoulder
Solar Plexus
Bronchial Area
Liver
Stomach
Gall Bladder
Pancreas
Adrenal Gland
Transverse Colon
Kidney
Ascending Colon
Lymphatic Drainage
Thoracic Vertebrae
Small Intestines
Ileo Cecal Valve
Bladder
Appendix
Lumbar and
Sacral Vertebrae
Right Knee
Collyx
Right Foot
Sciatic Nerve
Rectum

REFLEXOLOGY POINTS ON RIGHT FOOT

too weak to respond to the strong stimulation of acupuncture, or when the patient has a chronic fear of needles.

FOOT ZONE THERAPY (Reflexology)
Many parts of the body are recognised by practitioners as 'acupuncture microsystems'. That is to say, they reflect the entire body in one small area. The ears, eyes, nose, tongue, hands and feet have been particularly studied in this (charts

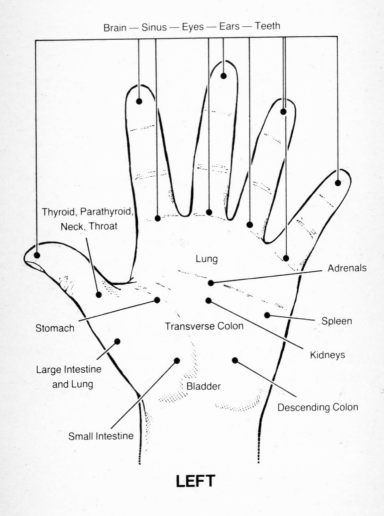

LEFT

REFLEXOLOGY POINTS ON LEFT HAND

showing points on the ear, hands and feet are illustrated pp. 19-22). The eyes are not used for treatment, though some possibility of treating the eye reflexes with laser light has been recognised. They are mainly used for diagnosis (this is known as iridology) and can tell practitioners a great deal about the body's state of health.

Massage is the traditional method of treating the reflex areas on the hands and feet and this treatment has come to be known

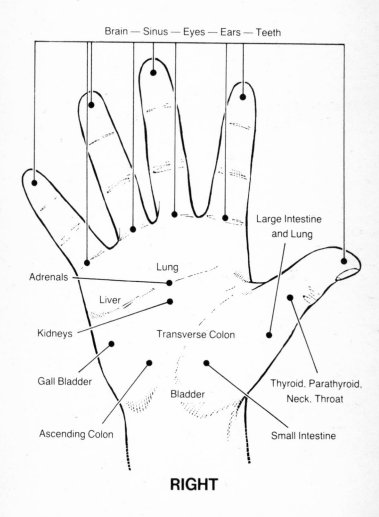

RIGHT

REFLEXOLOGY POINTS ON RIGHT HAND

as reflexology. Problems are usually detected by finding an increased sensitivity over the area. Sometimes it is possible to find small crystals which can be broken down by massage (this is usually done by pressing with the corner of the tip of the thumb).

Foot reflexology is not difficult to learn and practise oneself, or with the help of a friend. By relating the sensitive spots you find to the reflexes shown in the diagram, it is quite a simple matter to discover the area of the body which is at fault. In fact, regular treatment of the reflexes will encourage general healing of the whole body to take place in any case.

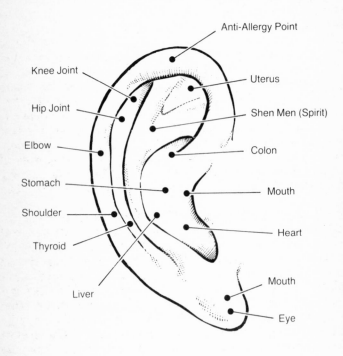

Anti-Allergy Point
Knee Joint
Uterus
Hip Joint
Shen Men (Spirit)
Elbow
Colon
Stomach
Mouth
Shoulder
Thyroid
Heart
Liver
Mouth
Eye

ACUPUNCTURE POINTS ON RIGHT EAR

OSTEOPATHY

Osteopathy is a system of medicine based on the belief that if the structure and alignment of the body are correct, then it will function properly. The body's structure and functions are inter-related, so that faulty structure may produce functional disorder and functional disturbance may, in its turn, affect the structure. Most osteopaths agree that functional problems can arise from poor nutrition, negative emotions and environmental pollution as well as from structural problems.

The joints and bone structure of the body can be disturbed by many things, including poor posture, colds, infection, lack of exercise, obesity, malnutrition or trauma. The connective tissue may become infiltrated by toxins as a result of lymphatic congestion, toxins in food and the air, metabolic disorder or trauma. Osteopaths are mainly concerned with joint mobility and look for diminished movement as the sign of a lesion. As well as the obvious movements which every joint makes, there are also hidden movements sometimes known as 'joint play'. These are tiny movements or degrees of tolerance which have to exist in every healthy joint. When these are diminished or absent, the osteopath can restore them by gentle manipulation. Even the joints of the skull are known to have movements of remarkable complexity which are now recognised by osteopaths. Manipulation of the bones in the head is known as craniopathy.

HOW DOES AN OSTEOPATH TREAT THE PATIENT?

An osteopath treats the patient by first testing all the relevant joints for normal movement and checking if there is any stiff-ness, pain or lack of mobility. Too much movement can also be found — this is usually caused by repeated over-stretching of ligaments or by a lack of certain nutrients, such as calcium fluoride and manganese. The osteopath searches at the same time for abnormally hard or soft tissue. Inflammation may be found by looking for discolouration or very small differences of surface temperature. Other important factors are: how the patient stands, sits and walks; how they get up and sit down; how rigid or relaxed their body appears generally.

Trigger spots are often found in relation to different joints. These are spontaneously sensitive points where one often finds tiny grain-like tissues. They correspond with certain acupuncture points and can be treated by massage or by acupuncture. Muscular balance is sought by the osteopath, who uses deep neuro-muscular massage to achieve this end. Sometimes, the osteopath will manipulate a joint either with gentle springing movements or by a specific high velocity thrust. It is also true that certain relatively minor aspects of the patient's lifestyle may be causing unnecessary problems and the osteopath may well point these out — for example, sitting in too low an armchair, wearing high-heeled shoes or constantly carrying heavy shopping in one hand. Little effort is required to alter these habits and the relief may be considerable.

If the potential problems are serious, the osteopath may also recommend a course of training in the Alexander Technique, a process of gradual relaxing, through exercise, to align the body correctly. To find an Alexander Technique teacher in your area, consult one of the associations listed on p. 188.

WHAT CONDITIONS CAN BE TREATED?
Osteopathy is mainly used for musculo-skeletal problems and particularly backache. However, because of the importance of the spine and the fact that it controls so many of the nerve impulses going to and from the various parts of the body, an osteopath is often able to treat diseases which may not be thought to have any musculo-skeletal involvement. It was demonstrated some time ago that osteopathic manipulation could help the body's immune system, so it is not an absurd idea to think that an osteopath should even treat a disease like measles or whooping cough. Very often correct spinal manipulation will enable the body to throw off the disease more easily.

Of course, the osteopath will always combine the treatment with sensible dietary advice and often with hydrotherapy (see opposite), for maximum effect. In general, osteopathic treatment improves the body's structure and makes the patient feel better. The treatment itself is occasionally a little painful when sensitive muscles are being deeply massaged, but generally pleasant and enjoyable.

Osteopathy should always be carried out by a qualified practitioner and indeed, would be very difficult to practise on oneself! It is recommended throughout the A-Z section which follows (p. 27 onwards), for chronic complaints or conditions which do not respond to other treatment.

However, gentle massage of the back and shoulders can be carried out at home and is particularly useful with stress-related problems.

HYDROTHERAPY

Hydrotherapy uses a number of traditional treatments involving water, particularly extremes of heat and cold. Examples are given below, and recommended in the A-Z section which follows.

COLD COMPRESS

You will need a basin or pail of ice cold water and two cloths such as small towels or old linen.

How to do it:

Soak one piece of towel in the cold water. Wring it out gently so that it no longer drips. If applying it to the face or chest do not fold, but apply one layer only. If applying it to other parts of the body, fold it until you have a suitable size to cover the area completely. Replace every few minutes if applied to the face or chest.

In very acute cases, e.g. sprains, a single compress may be applied every few minutes. In other cases cover with another piece of towel or cloth, bind firmly into position, and replace every twenty minutes or half hour.

At night, leave on overnight and spray the area with cold water when you remove it in the morning.

Always dry the area after treatment.

(A few drops of arnica montana Ø may be added to the water in cases of bruising or sprain.)

Benefits:

Prevents or relieves congestion; reduces inflammation; reduces fever; stimulates microcirculation; relieves pain.

Used for:

Inflamed joints, e.g. arthritis; sprains; fever; many respiratory conditions; headache and congestive conditions of the head.

HOT COMPRESS

This is made the same way as the cold compress, except that very hot water is used. A hot compress must always be replaced every few minutes. It can be used for the same conditions and ailments. Hot and cold compresses may also be alternated.

Benefits:

Tonic and sedative effects; improves circulation and sweating; dilates blood vessels; relaxes muscles; relieves pain.

SITZ BATH

You will need one or two tubs large enough to sit in and one or two foot tubs.

How to do it:
Fill one large tub with water as hot as can be tolerated. Fill the foot bath with very cold water and place it in front of the tub. Have the patient sit in a tub with their feet in the foot bath for five minutes. The water should just cover the hips and half the thighs. Knees are out of the water. Keep the water in the as hot as possible.

Now switch to the other tub (or refill the same tub) with ice cold water and place the feet in a hot foot bath. This should be done for two minutes.

The procedure may be repeated once or twice according to the strength of the patient.

Benefits:
Stimulates pelvic circulation and musculature of bowels, bladder and uterus; decongests pelvic organs.

Used for: Constipation; menstrual disorders; impotence and infertility.

A-Z OF COMMON AILMENTS

This alphabetical list of common ailments, and the First Aid section which follows it, should be used as a reference to the treatments you can apply yourself, when to consult a practitioner for further help, and when to use the treatments in conjunction with conventional treatment — for example, for broken bones, or after an anti-tetanus injection.

Note: the following abbreviations have been used for measurements: g — gram; mg — milligram; tsp — teaspoon; tbsp — tablespoon.

ACNE

What is it?
An eruption of spots on the skin, caused by overactivity of the sebaceous glands. Acne is usually found on the face, neck and back.

What are the causes?
- Probably excess androgen or oestrogen activity, which causes the oil-producing glands in the skin to secrete too much oil.
- Congestion of the liver. It may even be caused by falling in love! The strong emotion brings on a natural cleansing process of the liver.
- It may be aggravated by stress.
- In young girls it may accompany delayed menstruation, resulting from hormone imbalance.
- It may be aggravated by dairy products and sugar, and some cosmetics cause an allergic reaction.
- It may be due to nutritional deficiencies — especially vitamin A and zinc.
- The formation of blackheads is due to a build-up of pigmented cells blocking the hair follicle and has nothing to

do with dirt. Whiteheads are plugs of white blood cells which come to the surface.

What are the symptoms?
Appearance of spots and skin disturbance as above, particularly spots which do not die down in a few days, or which spread rapidly over the surrounding area, causing inflammation and irritation.

Who can get it?
Common acne affects mostly teenagers, but sometimes it continues into adulthood. There are other, rarer forms of acne which affect older people and children and are due to hormone problems and other factors.

Prevention
- Eat a healthy diet without refined carbohydrates or unnecessary additives, and as free from dairy products and sugar as possible.
- Do not smoke.
- Take plenty of exercise in the fresh air.
- Be happy! As with most skin problems, acne is always made worse by worry or unhappiness.
- Use hypo-allergenic cosmetics if possible.

Treatment
- Good bowel movement and a healthy bowel are absolutely essential in order to avoid toxic build-up in the bowel, which makes circulation sluggish. If constipated, take a tbsp of castor oil with orange juice. A daily supplement of acidophilus (available in tablet form or in live yogurt) is recommended.
- Liver cleansing (see p. 186) is also helpful.
- Calcium sulphate and magnesium phosphate dissolved in a glass of warm water is a good remedy to improve bowel health.
- Take a supplement of zinc orotate (50 mg a day) and selenium (200 mg a day), with professional supervision.
- Eat plenty of fresh fruit and vegetables. Reduce your intake of sugar, tea, coffee and dairy products.
- Have yourself checked for allergies or food intolerance.
- Avoid using greasy products on the skin. However, a mixture of essential oils of cajeput, lavender and juniper, massaged into the skin last thing at night, may help.
- Learn to cope better with stress (see p. 35).
- Take a supplement of vitamin A (100,000 IU) and vitamin

E daily (800 IU). This should be reduced as the condition improves.

- Wash the skin regularly, either without soap or with a neutral soap such as an oatmeal soap. Do not rub the skin, but pat it dry.
- Suggested homeopathic remedies:

Calcium phosphate: for girls who also suffer from anaemia during puberty.

Kali bromatum: the principal remedy for acne.

Asterias rubens: a remedy for red pimples on side of nose, mouth and chin.

Berberis aquifolium-mahonia: especially helpful for girls. Take two drops twice per day.

Tuberculinum: for tubercular children.

Dulcamara: if pimples occur before monthly periods.

Pulsatilla nigricans: when there is menstrual disorder.

Antimonium crudum: when there are many infected spots on the face. Usually accompanied by disgestive disorder and a white, dry coating on the tongue.

Arsenicum album: when pimples are hard and do not ooze. The remedy may be combined with sulphur. In this case take arsenicum in the morning and sulphur at night.

Psorinum: for severely infected acne which may be painful and accompanied by itching.

Radium bromide: useful if other remedies fail.

ADDICTION — see SMOKING, RELATED CONDITIONS

AIDS (Acquired Immune Deficiency Syndrome)

What is it?

A breakdown of the body's natural immune system brought about by numerous factors, which allows the replication of the retrovirus HIV III.

The condition is related to the HIV virus, but it would seem that a sizeable infection is needed. Although saliva and other body fluids contain the virus they do not appear to cause transmission of the disease. The only fluids at present known to be responsible for transmission of the virus are blood, semen and vaginal secretions. There is a risk, therefore, following unprotected sexual intercourse or the introduction of blood into the body by transfusion, or sharing contaminated hypodermic needles. AIDS can also be passed from a mother to her unborn baby.

On current advice, it would seem shortsighted to regard the transmission of the virus alone as the causative factor in AIDS. It is clear that frequent drug taking (including tobacco, alcohol and medically prescribed drugs), a depressed mental state, excessive sexual activity (male ejaculation causes zinc depletion and zinc is one of the essential elements for a healthy immune system) and the general consumption of junk or over-refined foods play an important part in the development of this disease. The combination of these and other adverse factors may, ultimately, pave the way to the transmission of the infection. It would also seem, on present evidence, that *repeated* infections may be required for the disease to become established.

Other factors which have been suggested are genetic make-up, vaccinations, gastrointestinal changes and candida albicans infection.

It is important to note that many of those who are infected and produce HIVIII antibodies do not go on to develop AIDS. Conversely, in many cases of the disease, it has not been possible definitely to establish the presence of the virus.

What are the symptoms?
There are really no early specific symptoms, although a cough, loss of weight and swelling of the lymph glands are fairly characteristic. Once the virus has taken hold the patient succumbs to a variety of opportunistic infections which normally would be fought off without symptoms. Forms of cancer and pneumonia are common in the late stages of AIDS, when the immune system is breaking down.

Unfortunately, AIDS is a progressive disease which eventually leads to the destruction of brain cells.

Who can get it?
Anyone who has unprotected sexual intercourse with an infected person is at risk. It is virtually non-existent in people between five and 15 years old. It is completely untrue to say that AIDS is a 'gay' disease — in Africa it is almost entirely confined to heterosexuals.

Prevention
Obviously, the most effective way of preventing the disease is to limit sexual intercourse to one partner. If this is not reasonable, the following precautions should be taken:

- Limit your number of sexual partners as much as possible.
- Never have unprotected sex outside a stable relationship. Men should use a condom.
- Refrain from anal intercourse.
- Avoid sexual contact near areas where there is any damage to the skin, e.g. cuts and grazes.
- Avoid taking drugs and *never* share a hypodermic needle.
- Ensure that you have a good nutritious diet and consider taking the supplements listed below.

Treatment

- Boost the body's immune system by taking a daily supplement of zinc, iron, copper, magnesium, selenium and vitamins A, E, B5, B6, B12 and folic acid.
- Take large doses (5-20 g) of vitamin C every day. As in all viral infections, it should be taken in a dose high enough to produce diarrhoea at first, after which the dose should be slightly reduced.
- Take Vital Dophilus or Super Dophilus in tablet form to repopulate your bowel with healthy lactobacilli. The acidopholus culture occurs naturally in some forms of live yoghurt, but for higher doses take Super Dophilus tablets.
- Take L-arginine (500 mg, at least four times a day) half-an-hour before meals and at bedtime.
- Avoid taking antibiotics and other drugs.
- Ensure that your diet consists of unrefined carbohydrates and plenty of fruit and raw vegetables. Avoid, as far as possible, junk food, refined foods, foods with additives, tea, coffee and alcohol.
- General health-promoting activities, both physical and mental, are advocated. These include suitable recreation and meditation.
- Get professional help. Acupuncture, homeopathy, Chinese herbs and special treatments such as essential oils and snake venom have all shown some promise in the management of AIDS.
- The anti-viral agent AZT is worth considering since it has been proven to prolong life in this disease.

ANAEMIA

What is it?
Deficiency of haemoglobin (the oxygen-carrying pigment in the red blood cells) in the blood. Usually there is also a deficiency of red blood cells.

What are the causes?
- Defective red cells.
- Lack of iron. This results in insufficient red blood cells being produced. It may be due to poor absorption or inadequate diet.
- Bleeding profusely or over a long period, e.g. from some forms of colitis, accidents, heavy menstruation or haemorrhoids, bleeding ulcers or piles.
- Deficiency of vitamin B12 or of folic acid, resulting in a lack of red blood cells. This may be caused by poor diet, but is more often the result of a lack of a special enzyme essential for the utilization of vitamin B12.
- Heredity. There are certain inherited blood disorders such as sickle cell anaemia, thalassaemia etc., for which medical attention is essential.
- Pregnant women, or children going through growth periods, may be anaemic.
- There are numerous other causes such as deficiency of vitamins C, E and B6, alcoholism, intestinal parasites, lead or zinc toxicity, auto-immune diseases such as rheumatoid arthritis, bone marrow disease, chemotherapy, Addison's disease, and myxoedema. A vitamin B12 deficiency anaemia can arise when a strict vegetarian or vegan diet is followed if the gut flora are unhealthy. This may occur in someone who was previously eating meat or when certain drugs, such as antibiotics, are taken.

In all cases, however, a simple blood test will quickly indicate signs of anaemia and treatment can be started immediately.

What are the symptoms?
Tiredness, paleness, dizziness, headaches, depression, breathlessness, palpitations and, possibly, swelling of ankles.

Who can get it?
Iron deficiency anaemia mostly affects women, because of their monthly blood loss while menstruating, and to a lesser extent elderly people and some babies fed on cow's milk (cow's milk contains less iron than human milk or goat's milk). Pernicious

anaemia usually affects people over 40. Hereditary disorders are mostly confined to certain ethnic groups, e.g. Greeks, Italians and others from the Mediterranean region who suffer from thalassaemia — a condition where the red cells are defective.

Prevention
- Eat a varied, healthy diet, avoiding tea and coffee if possible.
- Avoid being constipated, thus reducing the risk of piles which may bleed and can cause anaemia.
- Avoid drugs containing aspirin, which irritates the lining of the stomach and may cause it to bleed for a period of time.
- Take plenty of iron in your diet — liver, kidney, eggs, dried apricots, pulses and leafy green vegetables (do not overcook) are all good. If possible take foods high in vitamin C (e.g. oranges, blackcurrants, green peppers) at the same meal, as iron absorption is helped by vitamin C.
- Consider taking daily supplements of vitamins B6 and B12, particularly if taking the contraceptive pill, if pregnant or if breastfeeding.

Treatment
- Eat a lot of raw fruit and vegetables. Bananas are particularly recommended, as they are rich in iron phosphate, a form which the body easily absorbs, and vitamin B6, which helps the body to use iron. Beetroot juice is also highly recommended. Some foods which are rich in iron are listed on p. 182.
- Iron supplements should only be taken with medical advice, and it must also be noted that iron has been a very over-prescribed remedy. It is better to follow a balanced diet, which should provide all the iron required. If iron is to be taken it should be in the form of iron phosphate combined with calcium phosphate. This can be obtained in a tissue salt combination, or in conventional form if there is severe anaemia.
- Take a daily supplement of vitamin C and of B6.
- Use an alternative method of contraceptive in place of the pill, as it depletes many vitamins and minerals from the body, including vitamin B6.
- In some cases the recolonization of the large intestine with lactobacilli is necessary. Taking acidopholus daily should help.
- Massage the body with essential oils of garlic, mugwort, camomile, mint, sage, lemon or thyme. A mixture of the last three is useful.

ANXIETY

What is it?
Anxiety is a fear of what *might* happen, and often has no reasonable cause. Depression is a reaction against something that has already occurred. The two are frequently connected.

What are the causes?
Psychological causes, often dating back to childhood, frequently give rise to adult anxieties. Excessive caffeine (found in tea and coffee) and alcohol poison the nervous system and can aggravate anxiety. Low blood sugar can induce mental problems, as can nutritional deficiencies.

What are the symptoms?
Rapid heart beat, pounding of heart or palpitations, muscle tension, abdominal discomfort, insomnia, feeling depressed and low, sweating and tearfulness are common symptoms of anxiety but may be scarcely noticeable in some cases. In severe cases there may be panic attacks, when these symptoms are more marked and the patient may be very alarmed. Severe cases of anxiety are often termed phobias. Common phobias are agoraphobia (fear of open spaces and of going out), claustrophobia (fear of enclosed spaces, such as trains or lifts), acute fear of flying, spiders, etc.

Who can get it?
Generally, anxiety is a problem that affects adults, and is more prevalent amongst women than men. Anxiety neurosis is very rare in pre-pubertal children and 'school phobia' is commonest in the 12-15 years age group.

Prevention
- Follow a healthy diet with adequate vitamin B complex, calcium and magnesium.
- Drink minimal tea, coffee or alcohol and do not smoke.
- Take adequate exercise in the fresh air.
- A calm attitude of mind should be strived for — yoga, meditation and relaxation exercises are all helpful.
- If you have long-standing worries or fears, talk to a professional counsellor or therapist.

Treatment
- Tranquillizing and anti-depressant drugs are not recommended as they mask the real problems and often have side

effects which can cause more problems than they solve. The following natural methods should help you to deal with your anxiety without such drugs:

- Take 1 g of calcium and 250 mg of magnesium a day.
- Take 50 mg of vitamin B6 two or three times a day, plus a daily dose of vitamin B complex.
- Take L-glutamin (1-6 g) daily and L-tryptophan (500 mg) two or three times a day, both with water or fruit juice, at least half an hour before meals.
- Potassium phosphate, sodium phosphate and magnesium phosphate, as homeopathic tissue salts, are helpful.
- Regularly massage the acupoints Co 4 (hegu), Gv 20 (baihui), P 6 (neiguan), GB 34 (yanglingquan), Li 3 (taichong) and H 7 (shenmen). (See p. 165).
- Massage the neck, back and shoulders with any of the following essential oils: basil, bergamot, thyme, camomile, geranium, lavender, cedarwood, juniper, marjoram and frankincense. A judicious blending of a number of these suited to the individual is an excellent treatment. The essential oils should be dissolved in a carrier oil (any kind of vegetable oil — almond and sunflower are good). Foot zone massage, by a qualified reflexologist, may also be helpful.
- Acupuncture, acupressure and homeopathy are very helpful in cases of anxiety and depression. Phobias are more difficult to deal with but often respond well to psychotherapy treatment.
- Any form of relaxation, such as meditation or yoga, is to be encouraged. There are also numerous relaxation tapes available.

FORMS OF MEDITATION

There are many forms of meditation, and beginners would do well to consult a qualified teacher or read one of the many books on the subject before taking it up.

The basic principle of meditation is that you clear your mind of all worrying and disturbing thoughts by 'blanking' your mind and keeping your body perfectly still.

The state is more difficult to achieve than it may sound, but when correctly practised, meditation can bring excellent results to anxiety sufferers.

Three suggested positions for meditating are shown in the illustration overleaf. They are: sitting upright on a chair (not an armchair), lying flat on the ground (not a bed), or cross-legged on the floor, in the lotus position if you can manage it.

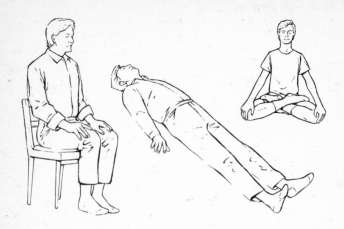

SUGGESTED MEDITATION POSITIONS

- Suggested homeopathic remedies:
  Acarite: for strong feelings of fear.
  Pulsatilla: for the 'emotional' type who cries and angers easily.
  Arsenicum album: for the fussy, restless worrier.
- The Bach Flower remedies (see p. 14) can be very helpful for many types of anxiety and depression. It is best to consult a qualified practitioner — e.g. a naturopath — for an initial diagnosis.
- Anxious people are often physically tense and do not breathe properly, while people who are depressed tend to 'slump' and display bad postural habits. In both cases, the Alexander Technique (see p. 24) can have remarkable effects.

APOPLEXY — see STROKES

APPENDICITIS

What is it?
An inflammatory condition of the appendix, which is a small part of the intestine, normally about the size of a little finger, with a blind ending. It has no function nowadays, although it may have had a use in the body many years ago.

What are the causes?

Appendicitis is a relatively modern problem, occurring when people adopt a Western 'civilized' diet. It was unknown amongst Africans until they began to eat refined foods, and even now is still very rare in rural Africa and other parts of the world where unrefined grains form the major part of the diet.

What are the symptoms?

The symptoms of appendicitis are: pain in the abdomen which starts in the centre and moves to the lower right side, rigidity of the muscles and tenderness over the area, slight fever and nausea. There may be vomiting (usually only once) and there is almost always constipation, though this may alternate with diarrhoea.

Who can get it?

Anyone, but mostly those between the ages of two and 30.

Prevention

Prevention is obviously the real answer to the problem, and this is a very simple matter: merely avoid refined foods and eat a diet high in fibre.

Treatment

The consequences of appendicitis can be very serious and expert medical advice is always necessary in cases of this condition. Surgical removal of the appendix is the standard treatment, but this is in fact often quite unnecessary and now less fashionable than in previous years. There are often repeated smaller episodes which do not last long and usually culminate in a severe, life-threatening attack. These 'mini' attacks are often known as a 'grumbling' appendix. Suggested treatment for these attacks is as follows:

- Immediate bed rest.
- Apply a cold compress to the painful area of the abdomen. In less severe cases alternate hot and cold compresses may be used. A hot compress or fomentation may also be applied to the spine (see p. 25).
- Careful massage to the descending colon (left side of the abdomen) should be given. This will encourage the movement of waste material along the colon.
- Give a foot massage with special attention to the appendix, intestine and colon reflexes (see p. 19).
- A fruit juice fast for several days is important, followed by a raw fruit and vegetable diet for a few more days. When normal eating is reintroduced the diet should exclude

refined carbohydrates and should contain a good proportion of whole grains. Ideally, the diet should be vegetarian.

- Take the homeopathic remedy belladonna every four hours. Dissolve the tablet in a little warm water and sip slowly.
- Slippery elm is extremely helpful for intestinal problems and may be taken once or twice a day. It is readily available in powder form from health food stockists and chemists.
- Contrast bathing and sitz baths are recommended as regular treatments to strengthen the abdomen after the initial symptoms have subsided (see p. 25).
- Certain yoga postures are very beneficial to the intestine and help to prevent constipation and appendicitis, but note that these postures should *not* be practised whilst there is any pain. The most useful postures are pavanmuktasana, jathara parivartanasana and uddiyana bandha (see pp. 180-181.)
- There is a special acupoint for appendicitis just below the knee (see p. 177); other important points are: St 36 (zusanli), Co 4 (hegu), Gv 20 (baihui), St 25 (tianshu) and Ren 12 (zhongwan) (see p. 165).
- Osteopathic manipulation may also be helpful.

ARTERIAL DISEASE (ARTERIOSCLEROSIS and ATHEROSCLEROSIS)

What is it?
Arteriosclerosis is a hardening of the walls of the arteries with a laying down of calcium deposits, which results in high blood pressure (see p. 106). The term is frequently used to include atherosclerosis and other arterial diseases. In atherosclerosis fatty deposits are found in the artery walls. This may in time affect the heart or brain leading to a heart attack, coronary heart disease, strokes (cerebro-vascular episodes) or senile dementia (Alzheimer's disease).

What are the causes?
There is a great deal of misunderstanding about the cause of arterial disease and its relation to the heart. The idea that it is caused by cholesterol is one of the principal misconceptions. In fact, normal serum cholesterol levels are frequently found in cases of heart disease and low cholesterol does not prevent it. The real causes of heart disease are the substances which

damage the walls of the arteries and these are:
- Tobacco smoking.
- 3-methyl cholanthrene, a toxic substance produced by hard, constipated stools which have been in the bowel for a long time.
- Chlorine from drinking water and other environmental toxins.
- Deficiencies of certain nutrients such as vitamin C, choline, vitamin E and magnesium.
- Excess saturated fats.
- Refined or fried foods.
- Lack of exercise.
- Excess salt may be a cause in some people.
- High blood pressure (see p. 106).
- Obesity.
- Deficiency of chromium is known to be a contributory factor.

What are the symptoms?
These vary according to the condition which develops — for example, see symptoms listed under 'Strokes', p. 134.

Who can get it?
Older people are more prone to arteriosclerosis as it is a common symptom of ageing. Atherosclerosis is more likely in those who are overweight, who smoke or are diabetic.

Prevention
- Do not smoke.
- Keep to your correct weight.
- Take regular exercise.
- Avoid stressful situations, or take steps to deal with them properly.
- Cut down on saturated animal fats.
- Cut down on alcohol consumption.
- Have your blood pressure checked regularly.
- Hawthorn tea is believed to aid high blood pressure by regulating the action of the heart.

Treatment
- Take a supplement of 1-3g of vitamin C a day. This activates a fat-splitting enzyme which initiates the removal of atheromatous plaques (sticky deposits which form on the walls of the arteries. Over a period of time these will cause narrowing of the blood vessels, leading to high blood pressure and, possibly, heart disease). Vitamin C should be

accompanied with bioflavonoids (vitamin P). They occur naturally together in foods such as citrus fruit and black-currants and work together in the body.

- Take a minimum of 500 mg vitamin E, which helps to prevent the strong adhesion of fatty deposits and clot form-ation. Vitamin E should be accompanied by selenium, which increases the vitamin's effectiveness.
- Other helpful supplements are lecithin, L-carnitine and dolomite.
- Supplements of kelp, dolomite, choline, inositol, vitamins B3, B5, B6, B complex, F, calcium, iodine, magnesium, phosphorus, silicon and chromium may help. Consult a naturopath for the most suitable selection for you.
- Take a supplement of brewer's yeast every day. It is a valu-able source of chromium, which is an ideal preventive against atherosclerosis. It also assists the high density lipo-proteins (HDL) which actually protect against heart disease.
- Drink bottled, filtered or boiled water only — not untreated tap water.
- Reduce your weight if you need to.
- Do not smoke and avoid smoky atmospheres.
- Eat a predominantly vegetarian diet and ensure that you have plenty of fibre. Make a drastic reduction in sugar consumption.
- Replace polyunsaturated fat in your diet with mono-unsaturated oils such as olive oil or peanut oil.
- Take four kelp tablets and two dolomite tablets per day.
- Yoghurt, buttermilk or cultured milk, all of which will reduce the level of cholesterol in the blood, should be taken on a daily basis.
- Garlic reduces triglycerides, serum cholesterol and the 'stickiness' of the blood platelets which cause the blood to clot. It also lowers blood pressure. At least two raw cloves of garlic, or odourless garlic capsules, should be taken each day.
- Take regular exercise, building up to about 20 minutes per day, so that the cardiovascular system is gently stretched. Take care to build up slowly and seek professional advice if possible.
- Appropriate acupoints for arterial disease are: baihui (Gv20), neiguan (P6), shenmen (H7) and shaochong (H9). (See p. 165)
- It is worth having a foot massage two or three times per week. This may also include the use of essential oils — garlic, lemon and juniper are all good for arterial conditions.

ARTHRITIS

What is it?
Arthritis is a word which describes a number of very different conditions, mainly affecting the bones and joints. The two principal types are rheumatoid arthritis (RA) and osteoarthritis (OA). Sometimes the latter is called degenerative joint disease (DJD).

Rheumatoid arthritis tends to affect women aged between 35 and 50, is more often found in the small joints, and at the outset the individual may feel generally unwell. In this type of arthritis the membranes around the joint become inflamed and thickened. Muscular irritation and bone distortion are common.

Osteoarthritis, on the other hand, tends to affect older people and occurs more often in the weight-bearing joints such as the knees and hips. The cartilage which protects the bony surfaces begins to wear away and, eventually, the bone itself begins to erode. Often there are projections of bone in and around the joint.

What are the causes?
- Poor diet, especially if large amounts of refined carbohydrates and sugar are consumed.
- Eating a lot of acid forming food (see p. 185) — increased acidity generally encourages arthritis. Gout often results from the formation of monosodium urate crystals which are derived particularly from meat. Their elimination is inhibited by alcohol.
- Excess alcohol, which injures the kidneys and prevents the excretion of uric acid, is a cause of OA and of gout.
- Poor digestion, excess saturated fats, obesity, constipation, hormonal imbalance and lack of exercise are all thought to be contributory factors.
- Smoking increases the toxic load in the body and probably contributes to arthritis. It also diminishes the vitamin C levels in the blood and affects other nutrients, lack of which can cause arthritis.
- Food allergies — citrus fruits and dairy products often provoke arthritis.
- Tea and coffee drinking also rob the body of valuable nutrients and this may pave the way for arthritis.
- Adverse emotions which seem to be associated with arthritis are anger and a wish for revenge. Often there is an ongoing emotional conflict. Certain people are prone to these emotions and the Bach Flower remedy Holly has been

shown to be very helpful in these cases. Emotions, of course, should not be suppressed, but negative emotions — and their physical consequences — do not thrive if the positive emotions and attitudes of love, forgiveness and tolerance are cultivated.

What are the symptoms?

Pain and stiffness of the affected joints. In OA the onset is slow and there is increasing pain and enlargement of the joint. Often, the joint is stiff and feels 'gritty'. Usually the pain and stiffness are relieved when the joint is moved and the condition is sometimes worse in the morning after a night's rest. Occasionally, there are knobbly swellings over the joints at the ends of the fingers.

In RA the onset is fairly sudden, with swelling and inflammation of the joint. The joint may appear puffy and hot at times. There may be vague aches and pains before the joint starts to swell. RA may move from one joint to another.

Who can get it?

Mostly older people. RA affects more women than men (about four times as many). OA tends to affect more men than women and the peak age group is 40-60.

Prevention

- Follow a good diet, with no refined foods.
- Reduce tea, coffee, cocoa and alcohol consumption. Choose herb teas instead.
- Eat plenty of raw vegetables and fruit.
- If you feel you need to, take a nutritional supplement of minerals and vitamins (see 'Treatment', below.)
- Reduce the amount of fat in your diet.
- Ensure that there are plenty of foods rich in calcium, zinc and vitamin C in your diet (see pp. 183-185).
- Take regular exercise.

Treatment

- Follow the suggestions listed under 'Prevention', above.
- Eat a predominantly raw food diet.
- Take the following dietary supplements:
  Vitamin A (25,000 IU, once or twice a day).
  Vitamin C (3-5g a day).
  Vitamin B2 (20mg a day).
  Vitamin B3 (1-2g a day).
  Vitamin B5 (100mg, once or twice a day).
  Vitamin B6 (100mg, twice a day).

Vitamin B12 (100 mg a week).
Folic acid (500 mg a day).
Vitamin B complex (usually three tablets a day).
Vitamin E (500 mg a day).
Bioflavonoids (1 g a day).
Magnesium (500 mg a day).
Zinc (40 mg a day).

- Evening primrose oil is very rich in gamma linoleic acid, which helps to form the prostaglandin E1. This in turn reduces the inflammation of RA.
- A vegetarian diet is recommended, to which fish may be added if liked.
- Have yourself checked for allergies, and eliminate these if possible.
- Willow bark tea is good for arthritis as it helps to reduce inflammation.
- Gently exercise, or at least move, the affected joint regularly.
- Guard against cold and damp.
- In the early stages of arthritis when the joint is inflamed a cold compress (p. 25) should be applied. This should be left on all night and taken off in the morning.
- Avoid stress and emotional upsets.
- Maintain good posture.
- Essential oils of garlic, juniper, lavender, cajuput, sage and rosemary are useful for gently massaging the affected areas.
- Osteopathy, acupuncture and homeopathy are all useful for arthritis. Sessions of Alexander Technique (see p. 24) are also recommended. The chief homeopathic remedies for arthritis are bryonia and rhus toxicondendron. Bryonia is indicated more often for OA. Rhus tox is indicated for the hot, red painful lesions of RA. There are a large number of other homeopathic remedies, but the prescription of these is best left to the physician.
- A combination of the following tissue salts is often helpful: nat phos, mag phos, kali mur, ferrum phos, calc phos (or calc fluor) and silica.

ASTHMA

What is it?
Episodes of difficult breathing due to an involuntary reaction of the airways in the throat and lungs. They close up and make breathing very difficult.

What are the causes?
- There may be an inherited tendency towards asthma.
- Psychological factors — nervous stress and the suppression of emotions are often linked with it.
- Poor circulation.
- Allergies to many substances, e.g. house dust, paint, tobacco, dairy products, food additives.
- Excessive consumption of carbohydrates.
- Underlying low blood sugar.
- Weakness of the glands or physical exhaustion.
- Chest infections.
- Sudden exercise.

What are the symptoms?
Symptoms include sudden breathlessness with a feeling of tightness in the chest or throat and a feeling of suffocation, with difficulty breathing out. There is wheezing and often coughing. There may be sticky sputum. Attacks are most frequent at night and early morning.

Who can get it?
Asthmatic children are likely to have other allergies (e.g. hay fever, eczema), or to come from a family where there is a history of allergies. Late onset asthma, in adults, is often related to psychosomatic and psychological factors, and deep rooted emotional problems.

Prevention
In both types, 'Treatment' is perhaps more relevant as there is little that can be done to prevent either a child or an adult becoming an asthmatic. However, the likelihood of future attacks can be cut down by paying attention to the following:
- Keep children away from known or likely causes of allergy, e.g. cats, house dust, cut grass.
- Cut down on dairy products and wheat.
- Establish good breathing habits (the Alexander Technique is particularly helpful — see p. 24).
- Sort out deep rooted psychological problems.
- Obviously, do not smoke!

Treatment
- Stop smoking, if you still do.
- Avoid factors which cause the problem, such as house dust, animal fur, feather pillows, scents and, if possible, central heating.
- Try an elimination diet (see p. 187) for two days and

continue on a maintenance diet of predominantly raw fruit and vegetables.

- Try avoiding citrus fruits for a period to see if any improvement is noted.
- Foods rich in vitamin A (see p. 182) are helpful for maintaining good health in the throat, lungs and bronchial tubes.
- Take daily supplements of pangamic acid (vitamin B15) vitamin B6, B complex, vitamin E, vitamin C and bioflavonoids. Garlic capsules are also recommended.
- Avoid putting on unnecessary weight.
- Do not use aluminium cooking utensils — choose stainless steel instead. Aluminium is highly active when it comes into contact with some foods and may cause a harmful allergic build-up in the body.
- Practise special breathing exercises. Daily exercise in the fresh air is also important.
- Dairy products often seem to aggravate asthma and so these foods should be avoided. However, yoghurt, especially if made from goat's or sheep's milk, is often helpful.
- The following herbal mixture is recommended for asthmatics: one part cayenne, four parts Irish moss, one part each of Iceland moss, horehound, thyme, red clover and liquorice. Mix well, make a stronge infusion as if for herbal tea and take a teaspoonful four times a day.
- Acupuncture, osteopathy, aromatherapy massage, homeopathy and the Alexander Technique have all been proved to be beneficial for asthma. In each case, consult a professionally qualified practitioner.

If an asthma attack occurs, the following procedure should be followed:

1 Sit the patient up in bed or a chair.
2 Keep the patient relaxed and calm — don't fuss over them.
3 Get the patient to do some abdominal breathing exercises.
4 Apply strong stimulation to the acupoint tiantu (Ren 22) (see p. 174).
5 Apply a hot cloth to the chest and a hot water bath to the feet if practicable.
6 Use an inhaler only if absolutely necessary — they contain drugs which may have harmful side effects.
7 Call in professional help if the attack is very severe or prolonged.

ATHLETE'S FOOT

What is it?
A form of ringworm found specifically between the toes.

What are the causes?
Ringworm is an infectious fungus which is very contagious — in the case of athlete's foot, it is often caught in swimming-pool changing rooms.

What are the symptoms?
Itchy, red skin between the toes. The skin may peel and become painfully inflamed.

Who can get it?
Anyone. Athlete's foot is highly contagious.

Prevention
- Wear rubber sandals in communal areas, such as swimming-pool changing rooms or showers.
- Avoid wearing synthetic fabrics (e.g. nylon tights) next to the feet.
- Keep your feet clean and always dry carefully between the toes.

Treatment
- See advice under 'Prevention', above.
- If infected, use separate towels from the rest of the family, to avoid spreading the fungus.
- Apply calendula ointment daily.
- Keep feet clean and dry — use a little powder between the toes.
- Lemon juice or cider vinegar can be dabbed on the lesions, followed by honey.
- Increase your intake of vitamins A and C (see pp. 182-183).

BACKACHE

What is it?
A variety of conditions are accompanied by pain in the back. This may be continuous when it is caused by disease in the back

itself, when it is referred from some other part of the body or when it is caused by an infection. If it is a local problem of the spinal joints the pain is usually intermittent. In such situations it will normally come on instantly or over a period of several hours and is usually worse in certain positions.

What are the causes?

- Strain of the ligaments or tendons, or inflammation of the synovial fluid which lines the joints.
- Lateral curvature of the spine.
- Prolapse or dislocation of the intervertebral disc ('slipped disc').
- Infections such as tuberculosis and viral infections.
- Pressure on a nerve (sciatica).
- Changes to the bones, as in arthritis.
- Kidney stones — as kidneys are situated in the lower back, when the stones irritate the kidneys there will be localised pain.
- Bowel or intestinal problems.
- Bad posture when sitting, standing or working, or a sedentary lifestyle.
- Muscular imbalance from chills, sudden movements, undue fatigue, bad techniques of lifting and bending.
- Badly constructed or ill-fitting shoes, especially high heels.
- Nutritional deficiencies which prevent strong bone formation.
- Obesity puts a strain on the spine, as does pregnancy.
- Depression and emotional disorders — over a period of time, hunching the shoulders up and keeping the back slumped in a 'defeatist' position will cause the spine to sag.
- Finally, injuries or accidents can of course damage the spine. If you are in any doubt after an accident, see an osteopath as soon as possible.

What are the symptoms?

Pains in the back can vary from sharp, shooting pains to a dull aching or burning feeling. However, backache can be a symptom of numerous diseases and the pain may occur elsewhere in the body, according to the problem. The most common site for spinal pain is the low back, followed by the neck. Headache and leg pains are often caused by spinal problems. Knee pain is often the result of a lesion of the third or fourth lumbar vertebrae in the back.

Who can get it?

Anyone. Those whose jobs involve lifting and carrying heavy

objects are obviously particularly at risk, as are pregnant women, but see also list of 'Causes' on previous page.

Prevention

A great many incidents of back pain can be prevented, and this area responds very well to self-help.

First ensure that your posture is correct. You can check this by standing with your back to a wall, with heels, buttocks, shoulders and the back of your head against the wall. The lower back should be about one to two inches from the wall. Alternatively, lying flat on a firm surface, there should be the same gap (one to two inches) between the lumbar spine (lower back) and the surface you are lying on. This is the posture to aim for. When walking, keep your shoulders dropped but your head high — a good tip to remember is to pretend you have a piece of string attached to the top of your head, pulling you up from a source on the ceiling.

Make sure that when you are sitting, your back is straight with the lower back bent slightly forward. At work, make sure that you are not forced into a bad posture by the conditions at your work place. A desk and/or chair at the correct height are essential.

On waking in the morning, gently stretch the whole body for a couple of minutes before getting out of bed. When lifting a heavy object, keep it close to your body. If bending and lifting, make sure that you bend your legs and keep your back straight. Never lean over or lift anything at an angle: get directly in front of it, squat down and rise up with your back straight.

Exercise

The following exercises and those on pp. 50-51 are designed to promote flexibility and muscular balance. Practise as many of them as you wish, once a day.

Running on the spot

Do this for about two minutes. Run on the balls of the feet, not the toes. Keep loose.

Forward bending

Stand with feet about 18 inches apart and pointing forwards. Bend forward from the hips and keep the back as straight as possible. Place your fingers as low down the left leg as you can comfortably reach. Do not try to touch your toes, but if you can do so, all the better! With gentle rocking movements, push the hands slowly further down, six to ten times. Repeat with the other leg.

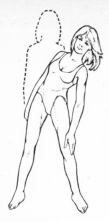

Side bending
Stand with feet apart and hands by sides. Bend to the left and let the left hand slide down the side of the left leg. Do not bend forward. Straighten up and repeat 10 times, then repeat on right side.

Shoulder stretch
Stand as in previous exercise, with elbows raised to shoulder height. Push the elbow backwards with gentle thrusts as if trying to make them touch behind your back. Do the same thing with the arms outstretched sideways, and the palms facing forwards. Repeat several times.

Hip stretch
Stand with feet together and hands on hips. Stretch your left leg out to the side as far as possible, keeping the foot on the floor, and bending the right knee. Repeat several times and then reverse legs.

Sit-ups
Lie on your back with knees bent and feet flat on the floor slightly apart, and as close to the buttocks as is comfortable. Clasp your hands behind the back of your head. Sit up, keeping your body facing the front. Repeat six times. Then repeat, with the body rotated first to the left and then to the right.

Side to side swings

Lie in the same position as for the sit-ups, but with the arms stretched out sideways. Push your knees towards the floor, alternating from one side to the other. Keep your knees as near to your chest as possible when starting each movement. Repeat several times.

Leg swings

Start in the same position as the previous exercise, but have your legs stretched up straight towards the ceiling. Swing your legs over to the right and then the left as far as possible, keeping shoulders and arms flat on the floor. Repeat three times on each side.

Pelvic roll

Start in the same position as for the sit-ups but with the arms at about 45° to each side, resting on the floor. Raise your hips, putting your weight on your shoulders, and rotate the pelvis in a circular fashion, first clockwise, then anticlockwise, 10 to 15 times in each direction.

Thigh stretch

Sit on the floor with your back straight and your legs stretched out as far as possible to each side. Lean forward from the hips as near to the floor as you can comfortably get, five times if possible.

Spine massage movement
Stand with feet slightly apart,
with your arms stretched above
your head and your hands
clasped. Exhale deeply and turn
your torso to the left, making
three complete circles in front of
the body. Swing your arms and
body down and around as you go.
Inhale during these movements.
Finish the set of three movements
in the starting position and exhale.
Repeat, rotating to the right, three
times as before.

Extensor exercise
Lie face down, with a pillow or
small cushion under your pelvis.
Clasp your hands behind your
back and raise the upper body,
bringing the shoulder blades as
close together as possible. Relax
slowly. Repeat 10 to 12 times at
first, building up to 20 if possible.

Treatment

- In many cases the simple exercises shown above and on the previous pages will be enough to relieve the pain. If in doubt, consult an osteopath.
- Massage the acupoints hegu (Co4), housi (SI 3) and the special points for low backache (see p. 165).
- Nutritional supplements which are useful are: manganese, magnesium, calcium, phosphorus, protein, vitamin B complex and vitamins C, D and E.
- Massage to the spinal reflexes on the foot is often helpful.
- Essential oils of camomile, geranium and lavender, singly or in combination, are good for backache. These may be applied to the soles of the feet or massaged into the back in a carrier oil such as almond or olive oil.
- A large number of homeopathic remedies are helpful. For spasmodic pains, magnesium phosphoricum is particularly useful.

BAD BREATH (HALITOSIS)

What is it?
An unpleasant odour coming from the mouth.

What are the causes?
Infections of the gums, teeth, nose, or throat, smoking, bad diet, poor digestion, food intolerances or allergies.

What are the symptoms?
Breath odour, but there may also be a bad taste in the mouth.

Who can get it?
Almost anyone.

Prevention
- Good mouth hygiene is vital. Teeth should be cleaned every day and dental floss used regularly to prevent particles of food becoming trapped between the teeth, decaying and causing odour.
- Avoid excessive consumption of sugar and refined carbohydrates, which cause tooth decay.
- Ensure that your diet contains sufficient vitamin A and take a supplement of vitamin C to maintain healthy gums and teeth.
- Reduce the amount of meat, dairy products and refined foods in your diet. Take plenty of fibre in the diet and deal with problems such as constipation, sinusitis, tonsillitis or gum disease.
- Try to breathe through the nose.

Treatment
- Bad breath should be seen as a symptom of an underlying problem, which needs to be dealt with and not just 'covered up' with breath fresheners and mouthwashes. It is important to eliminate any of the causes mentioned above and deal with any respiratory problems.
- Ensure that your liver and eliminative organs are working well. A general reflexology treatment may help with this. Otherwise consult a practitioner.
- A fruit or vegetable juice regime for a few days is often helpful in eliminating toxins and to cleanse the liver.
- Foods rich in chlorophyll, such as parsley, watercress and leafy green vegetables, help to absorb breath odour.

- Drink plenty of water but do not drink with meals, as fluids reduce the effect of the gastric juices. This can lead to mouth odour.
- Fully oxygenate your system with regular deep breathing.
- Do not smoke.
- Have yourself checked for any food intolerance or allergy.
- Chewing a clove or fennel seed helps to promote mouth health and imparts a pleasant smell to the breath.
- Deal with stress and anxiety if possible, as they often impair good digestion and thus may cause bad breath.

BEDSORES

What are they?
Bedsores are a particular type of skin ulcer caused by pressure over the bony areas of the body, restricting the circulation.

What are the causes?
Sitting or lying in the same position for long periods of time, causing continuous pressure on the same spots.

What are the symptoms?
Localised redness followed by inflammation and appearance of the ulcers. They occur particularly on the hips, buttocks, heels and shoulder blades.

Who can get them?
The elderly, paraplegics and those who lie immobile for long periods, e.g. the comatose.

Prevention
- Keep the person as mobile as possible under the circumstances.
- Use cushions or pillows to support the sensitive areas of the body and to keep them off the mattress.
- Regular massage is important, as is rubbing the body with alcohol (use rubbing alcohol, available from chemists) to stimulate the circulation.

Treatment
- Vitamins A, B2, C, D, E and copper are useful supplements.
- Calendula ointment should be applied at the first sign of any redness.

- Regular massage to encourage circulation is important.
- If there are open lesions, apply a gauze with honey. On the reverse side of the gauze place a crushed clove of garlic. Cover the gauze with dressing.
- Essential oils of sage, lavender and thyme may be used either for massage, in a carrier oil, or directly in a bath. Alternatively, try lovage or sage herbs in the bath — tie a small bundle of the dried herb into a muslin bag and let the bath water run over it.
- Suggested homeopathic remedies:
  Chamomilla: if patient is irritable, thirsty, hot and numb, and may have one cheek flushed.
  Fluoricum acidum: particularly useful if there is itching and a lumpy, vein-like appearance on the sores.
  Graphites: particularly indicated if the sores 'weep'.
  Petroleum: dry, cracked skin.
  Silicea: boils, suppuration and callosities.
  Sulphur: dry, scaly, unhealthy, itching skin with suppuration.
  Hypercal is a mother tincture combining hypericum perforatum and calendula officinalis. It can be used to bathe the sores — dilute five drops of hypercal in half a pint of water.

BEDWETTING
(NOCTURNAL ENURESIS)

What is it?
Many young children go through a period of bedwetting — the involuntary release of urine at night, while sleeping — but most of them grow out of it by the time they are four or five.

What are the causes?
Obviously, lack of bladder control is the immediate cause, and it may be triggered either by underlying emotional stress, or, less usually, by nerve irritation near the bladder, postural defects or an over-acidic diet.

What are the symptoms?
Obvious.

Who can get it?
Noctural enuresis is a childhood condition, usually in children

under five. Adult incontinence is a different condition and sufferers should consult a practitioner.

Prevention
As the condition is fairly common in young children, it is difficult to prevent it happening altogether. However, to lessen the likelihood of prolonged bedwetting once it has started, consider the following suggestions:
- *Never* punish a child for bedwetting accidents.
- Try to resolve any difficulties in the family, at school, etc., about which the child may be worrying.
- Make sure the child passes urine before going to bed, and take him/her to the toilet again when you go to bed.
- Encourage the child to wait for a little during the day before passing urine, to promote bladder control.
- Once you see signs of improvement, help to reassure the child by leaving a 'potty' under the bed for easy access.

Treatment
- Use great diplomacy so that you do not create or aggravate any psychological problem. Never express disapproval.
- One teaspoonful of pure unfiltered honey at bedtime helps the body retain water and promotes sound sleep.
- Switch to a predominantly alkali forming diet (see p. 185) — acid urine can be a cause of bedwetting.
- Make a tea with one tsp fennel seeds to a cup of boiling water. Allow to seep for five minutes and have the child sip it slowly at bedtime.
- Give the following Bach Flower remedies:
  Mimulus: where there is fear, shyness and timidity.
  Agrimony: where there is worry or when there are mental problems created by stress.
- Massage the acupoints zusanli (St 36), zhiyin (B1 67) (at the base of the nail of the little toe, on the outside), baihui (Gv 20), sanyinjiao (Sp 6), and guanyuan (Ren 4) which is four fingers' breadth below the navel.
- Massage the abdomen with essential oils of cypress and pine. Use a good carrier oil, such as almond oil, with twelve drops of essential oil to one fl. oz of carrier.
- Magnesium phosphoricum should be given three times per day for at least two weeks to improve the general neuro-muscular condition.
- The following homeopathic remedies may be used:
  Apis mellifica: If the urine is scanty and there is a lack of thirst.
  Causticum: for general bladder weakness. Often there is an

involuntary loss of urine when laughing or coughing. Bedwetting always occurs early in the night. The child is often clumsy.

Cina: for bedwetting during the full moon. Urine turns milky on standing. It can also be very useful if there is a worm infection.

Ignatia: for bedwetting from shock to the nervous system, especially when the child's pride is hurt.

Kalium phosphoricum: for hyperactive children with an irritable bladder. Bedwetting generally occurs during deep sleep.

Pulsatilla nigricans: for sensitive girls, who are afraid of the dark and of being left alone.

Sepia: when bedwetting occurs in first sleep. The child is a bad mixer and sulky.

Silicea: when bedwetting occurs in deep sleep.

Equisetum hyemale: when there is an associated infection.

Zincum: where there are suppressed emotions. Use in combination with the appropriate Bach Flower remedies (see p. 14).

- In prolonged cases or those involving older children, consider seeking the help of a trained counsellor or child guidance therapist.

Note: Incontinence in adults is a different condition, with different causes and treatments. Sufferers should consult a practitioner, and not attempt to treat themselves.

BOILS

What are they?

A boil is an infected area of skin and subcutaneous tissue which has a central core of pus and usually comes to a head from which it will discharge within a few days. It usually develops on a hair follicle or sweat gland.

A carbuncle, which is a collection of boils, invades the surrounding tissue. This can be dangerous because the bloodstream may become infected.

Boils may be an indication of a diabetic or pre-diabetic state, because high blood sugar provides the ideal condition for boils to develop. Boils in the nose may lead to blood poisoning and even meningitis.

What are the causes?
- Poor nutrition.
- Poor circulation.
- General toxicity which allows the resident bacteria to become pathogenic.
- Being 'run down'.
- High blood sugar levels, caused by diabetes.

What are the symptoms?
There is usually a local tenderness and hardness which later manifests as a dark red, hot and painful swelling. It ultimately begins to suppurate or discharge. There may be low-grade fever.

Who can get them?
In theory, anyone. There is some evidence to suggest that diabetics are more prone to boils.

Prevention
- Eat a good, wholefood diet with as little sugar and fatty foods as possible.
- Take regular exercise.

Treatment
- Take 25,000-50,000 IU of vitamin A and 1 g vitamin C per day for a week or until the boil has healed.
- Take zinc (50 mg a day) until the boil has healed.
- A three to seven day fast on fruit juice or vegetable juice is highly recommended. This may need to be extended or repeated. It should be followed for a few days by a fruit only diet.
- Subsequently, a good nourishing diet should be adopted, and sugar and refined foods excluded. Saturated fats, hydrogenated fats, fried food, chocolate and an acid-forming diet should be avoided.
- Tea tree oil may be applied at regular intervals. Alternatively, use a combination of essential oils of camomile, lavender, lemon, myrrh, and thyme.
- Suggested homeopathic remedies:
  Gunpowder: often used as a routine remedy.
  Lycopodium clavatum: for blind boils, which never come to a head.
  Arsenicum album: when there is chronic blood poisoning, fever, thirst for cold drinks, restlessness, anxiety and redness of the tongue.
  Belladonna atropa: in the early stages of development and when it is painful, hot and shining before suppuration.

Sulphur: if there are frequent boils.
Kali nitricum: when there is septic suppuration.
Mercurius sulphuricus: if the boil is putrid and suppur-
ating.
Hepar sulphuris calcareum: often helps to 'mature' the
boil and is also useful for dental abscesses.

BUNIONS

What are they?
An inflamed swelling on the side of the big toe, usually near its
base.

What are the causes?
Bunions are almost invariably caused by poorly fitting shoes
which push the toes together. Fashionable narrow-toed shoes are
frequent culprits.

What are the symptoms?
Initially, the bunion merely causes some discomfort, but if not
treated promptly it becomes painful as the inflammation
increases.

Who can get them?
Inevitably, women will be more prone to bunions as long as fashion dictates narrow-toed footwear for them!

Prevention
- Wear shoes which allow plenty of room for the toes.
- Do not wear very tight-fitting socks.
- Rest your feet whenever possible by walking around bare-
foot when indoors.
- Practise basic foot exercises — wiggle your toes!

Treatment
- Change to more comfortable footwear and remove shoes
whenever possible.
- Massage the feet regularly with oil — rosemary and lavender
are soothing.
- Gently manipulate the toe every day to prevent further
inflammation and stiffness.
- Bathe the feet in a solution of Epsom salts in reasonably hot
water.
- Alternated hot and cold water is also helpful.

BURSITIS

What is it?
An acute or chronic inflammation of a bursa. Bursas are small sacs filled with fluid situated between the tendons and bones around the joints. Their purpose is to prevent friction and damage.

What are the causes?
Knocks or bumps to the area, particularly when repeated, overuse (micro-trauma), poor diet, toxaemia, infection, gout or arthritis.

What are the symptoms?
Swelling, pain and limitation of movement. In chronic cases the wall of the bursa may become thickened and there may be muscular weakness.

Who can get it?
Mostly adults. Bursitis is frequently an occupational problem.

Prevention
Take a good nourishing diet. Vitamin C is particularly helpful in protecting against this kind of problem. Avoid repeatedly knocking or bumping any joint.

Treatment
- Apply a cold compress (see p. 25). Leave it on for about 20 minutes and replace if necessary. Repeat this process several times a day and leave the compress on overnight. Sometimes alternated hot and cold compresses are more effective, or in chronic cases, hot compresses alone.
- Mobilize the joint (it is best to get an osteopath or physiotherapist to do this).
- Apply essential oils of lavender, marjoram, eucalyptus and rosemary to the area. These should be mixed in equal quantities and massaged into the affected area. In an acute case 20 drops in a day may be applied either direct to the skin or in a carrier oil such as almond or olive oil.
- Homeopathic apis every two hours may be helpful when there is puffiness, redness and pain. In chronic cases rhus toxicodendron often gives relief.
- Take the following supplements:
  Vitamin A (25,000 IU, three times a day).

Brewer's yeast (one tsp, three times a day).
Vitamin C (1 g,, 6 to 12 times a day), plus bioflavonoids
(200 mg a day).
Vitamin E (200 mg, twice a day).
Calcium orotate (800 mg a day).
Magnesium orotate (400 mg a day).
- Other treatments such as acupuncture, lasertherapy or
  ultrasound are also recommended and most physical thera-
  pists can apply these.

CANCER

What is it?
The word 'cancer' is generally used to refer to a tumour, which
occurs when some of the normally healthy cells in the body start
to behave in an unnatural way — they change size and shape,
multiply rapidly and start to spread into other parts of the body.
As tumours can affect virtually every part of the body, there are
many different types of cancer with different causes and symptoms.

What are the causes?
The possible causes of cancer are far too numerous to list and
indeed have not all been discovered, or proven. However there is
little doubt that the following factors have links with different
types of cancer: radiation, asbestos and other pollutants; over-
exposure to sunlight, especially for those with pale skins; some
food additives, e.g. artificial colourants; smoking (a major
cause); obesity and constipation; a diet low in nutrients but high
in additives; constant stress or suppression of anger; excess
alcohol; genetic factors; certain major infections, such as the
AIDS virus.

What are the symptoms?
Any of the following signs and symptoms *may* indicate cancer,
but it is important to note that many of them are frequently
found in other conditions:
- There may be skin changes, such as the appearance of
  cracks (particularly on soles of feet and hands) and/or
  flaking of the skin around the abdomen and buttocks when
  rubbed with the open hand. The skin may take on a sallow
  or grey tone.

- The nails are hard, brittle, often ridged and crack or break easily.
- Hair tends to be dry and lifeless.
- Swelling of the leg above the ankle which displays dimples and is sore when pressed.
- An ulcer which does not heal.
- A wart or mole which becomes larger or changes in any way.
- Any unusual bleeding or discharge.
- A change in bowel habits, particularly constipation alternating with diarrhoea and/or blood in the stools.
- Gums bleed easily.
- Wounds which do not heal in usual time.
- Undue fatigue.
- Apathy — the patient becomes disinterested in things.
- Easy bruising.
- Unexplained loss of weight.
- History of cancer in family.
- Poor appetite.
- Hoarseness or a cough which lasts for several weeks.
- Difficulty in swallowing or persistent indigestion.
- A burning sensation in an area which feels quite cool to the touch.
- Burning sensation on passing a motion.
- Anaemia.
- Coughing up blood.
- Lumps, e.g. in the breasts.
- The early recognition of cancer is possible in some types — e.g. cervical cancer, via smear tests — and it is now possible to detect pre-cancerous cells from biopsies. However, diagnosis of many types of cancer is still difficult.

Who can get it?
Anyone. Certain cancers are age and sex specific. Obviously cancer of the prostate occurs only in men and usually only after the age of about 60.

Prevention
- Follow a healthy diet, with plenty of fresh fruit and vegetables. Cut down on salt, meat and fried food.
- Do not eat heavily smoked foods.
- Avoid food additives as much as possible.
- Check yourself regularly for lumps in the breasts and see a doctor if they appear.
- See a doctor if you have any unexplained bleeding or weight loss.
- Ensure that your diet contains adequate dietary fibre.

- Take supplements of selenium, zinc, vitamins A, C and E.
- Do not smoke and avoid passive smoking as much as possible.
- Reduce your alcohol consumption.
- Do not over-expose yourself to the sun, and never allow yourself to get sunburnt.
- Aim to be the correct weight for your height.
- Do not consume very hot food or drink.
- Women should have smear tests regularly to 'catch' precancerous cells before they develop.

Treatment
Although cancer is a frightening and undeniably serious illness, it often responds to holistic treatment (whereas chemotherapy and other conventional treatments have distressingly low long-term success rates and many unpleasant side effects).

- Take Ge 132 (organic germanium). Garlic, comfrey, ginseng and aloe are all rich in germanium.
- Cleanse the bowel and liver (see pp. 186-187).
- Eat only organically grown fruit and vegetables. A completely vegetarian diet is important, with *no* refined or processed foods or additives.
- Drink at least one pint of raw (fermented) beetroot juice per day.
- Take dietary supplements of selenium, zinc, magnesium and vitamins A, B6, C and E. At least 2 g of vitamin C a day is recommended.
- Do not take tea, coffee, alcohol or tobacco in any form.
- Herbal painkillers can bring relief and have no side effects.
- Homeopathy is often helpful — consult a qualified homeopath for advice.
- It cannot be stressed too strongly that the holistic approach to cancer requires a completely positive attitude of mind. It is therefore recommended that you visit a psychotherapist to deal with the situation and with any underlying feelings of guilt, anger, etc., which may prevent successful healing.
- Daily relaxation is important — meditation tapes are available (those by the healer Matthew Manning are particularly recommended).

CARBUNCLES — see BOILS

CARPAL TUNNEL SYNDROME

What is it?
The compression of a large nerve at the wrist, caused by swelling of the tissues in the wrist. When compressed, the nerve passes through a narrow 'tunnel' — hence the name.

What are the causes?
- Underactive thyroid.
- Overweight.
- Possibly fluid retention.
- Rheumatoid arthritis.
- Injury to the wrist.
- Pregnancy.
- Diabetes.

What are the symptoms?
Pain and tingling in the hand and fingers which may extend to the arm. Most often the thumb, index finger and thumb side of the ring finger are affected.

Who can get it?
The syndrome mostly affects middle-aged or pregnant women, and diabetics.

Prevention
- Keep to your correct weight.
- Deal with any fluid retention.
- Have a thyroid check if in doubt.
- Keep your diabetes under control.

Treatment
- Take vitamin B6 (50 mg a day). It may be necessary to persevere for several months.
- Take calcium phosphate 6× and silica 6×, every four hours. In some cases calcium fluoride may be more useful than calcium phosphate.
- If there is wasting of the thumb muscle or other signs of neurological damage, it is best to have surgery as soon as possible to release the nerve. In other cases, it is worth trying acupuncture.

CATARRH

What is it?
The production of excess mucus in the nose and throat. It is usually triggered by irritations or infections, and can be a side effect of many illnesses.

What are the causes?
It is caused by the mucous membranes of the nose and throat producing far more mucus than usual, in response to an attack by a virus or allergic substance. This excess mucus is what we know as catarrh.

What are the symptoms?
Typical symptoms are a blocked-up nose, headache, pain around the eyes, earache, coughing up mucus and a 'stuffed-up' feeling.

Who can get it?
Anyone, though some people may be more predisposed to having catarrh.

Prevention
- Don't smoke.
- Follow a diet which is fairly low in dairy products.
- Avoid known or potentially allergic substances.
- Keep your home and workplace well-ventilated.

Treatment
- Catarrh symptoms respond well to dietary changes. On a short-term basis it is necessary to spend a few days on an eliminative diet (see p. 187). This should be followed for one or two weeks by a diet which excludes the chief mucus forming foods. These are milk, milk products, eggs, meat, saturated fats, beans, peas, peanuts, grains and other carbohydrate type foods.
- On a permanent basis, try to avoid refined carbohydrates and junk foods. The proportion of fruit and vegetables in the diet should be increased.
- Overeating is a potent cause of catarrh. Try to reduce the quantity of your food, but improve the quality.
- Take fenugreek daily. This can be made into a tea by putting a teaspoonful of the dried seeds in a cup of boiling water. Alternatively, the powdered seed may be added to

your food, or can be taken in tablet form.
- Have an allergy test and thereafter avoid foods to which you are allergic.
- Avoid fried foods.
- Take regular daily exercise.
- Improve your liver function (see p. 186).
- Take regular supplements of vitamin C, alfalfa and garlic perles.
- Suggested homeopathic remedies:
  Hydrastis (morning and night): for all cases of catarrh.
  Ferrum phosphoricum: in the early stages.
  Gelsemium sempervirens: for catarrh in the summer season. Patient wants to lie down. Heaviness in the head.
  Pulsatilla nigricans: for the second and third stages of catarrh, when the discharge is thick.
  Nux vomica: for constipation, with one nostril blocked and a watery discharge during the day.
  Kalium bichromicum: for a thick yellow discharge, sore throat, hoarseness and tough, stringy mucus. There is often a cough which is worse in the early morning, between four and five a.m.

CHICKENPOX

What is it?
Acute, infectious disease of childhood.

What are the causes?
It is caused by the varicella virus, which is closely related to the herpes virus.

What are the symptoms?
Chickenpox usually starts with a rash which appears in crops of dark pink, flat spots which form blisters, then pustules and, finally, scabs. They tend to be on the trunk rather than the limbs, but may start on the mouth and head. There is fever and there may be a runny nose.

Who can get it?
Mostly children under 10 years old.

Prevention
Not generally possible once an epidemic has started.

Treatment

- See treatment of 'Fever', p. 92.
- Although chickenpox is usually a mild disease, it is very important to take it seriously and to treat it correctly, because occasionally in very young children it can be dangerous. The most important aspect is to stop normal feeding for a few days and go on an eliminative diet (see p. 187).
- Avoid scratching the spots. This is helped by wearing loose clothing, keeping cool, having a tepid bath with cider vinegar (half a cup of vinegar to a bath) and applying calamine lotion to the rash.
- Keep the child on fruit juice only for one or two days, or alternate between fruit and vegetable juice.
- Suggested homeopathic remedies:
  Rhus toxicodendrum: this is the best remedy for the disease and should be given unless there is a clear indication for another one.
  Aconitum napellus: useful during the early stage of eruption.
  Hepar sulphuris calcareum: for septic lesions aggravated by scratching.
  Sulphur: to reduce irritation and scratching.
  Pulsatilla nigricans: if the child is weepy but not irritable, worse in warmth, likes fresh air and has little thirst even during fever.

CHILBLAINS

What are they?
Small patches of inflamed, swollen skin, usually on the tips of the toes or the backs of the fingers.

What are the causes?
Chilblains are caused initially by bad circulation, which prevents adequate blood supplies reaching the extremities of the body (i.e. the fingers and toes). The resulting cell damage produces chilblains. They are aggravated by cold and damp weather.

What are the symptoms?
Small red or purple patches appear on the skin. They are itchy at first, then become painful.

Who can get them?
Anyone.

Prevention
- Keep your feet and hands warm and dry whenever possible in winter.
- Improve your circulation.
- Cut down on tea and coffee.
- Do not smoke.

Treatment
- Take daily supplements of calcium and eat plenty of calcium rich foods, especially yoghurt, almonds, sesame seeds, green vegetables and oranges.
- Take a supplement of vitamin B complex (500 mg a day) and vitamin C (500 mg a day).
- Avoid coffee, alcohol and tobacco and take as little tea as possible.
- Add one drop of iodine to a tumbler of water and sip throughout the day until the condition improves — in chronic cases this should be taken once a week; in acute cases it should be taken daily.
- Bathing in alternate hot and cold water helps to improve the circulation.
- Massage the toes with essential oils of lemon, onion and lavender.
- Paint the chilblains with tincture of myrrh once a day.
- Suggested homeopathic remedies:
  Agaricus muscarius: every three hours when the chilblains are more painful when cold.
  Rhus toxicodendrum: twice per day when chilblains are dusky red and burn a lot.
  Petroleum: when the chilblains are cracked (apply calendula ointment locally).
  Pulsatilla nigricans: every six hours when there is a tendency to chilblains which are worse when hot.

CHILDBIRTH — see FIRST AID SECTION

CHOKING — see FIRST AID SECTION

COLD SORES

What are they?
Small blisters which break out at the junction of the mucous membranes and the skin, often at the border of the lips. They are caused by the herpes simplex virus and are infectious. Genital herpes is a similar condition, which occurs in the genital area.

What are the causes?
The virus is very prevalent and may lie dormant in the system before becoming activated by stress, local irritation such as excessive sunlight, acid food or poor nutrition. Most people have the virus without symptoms.

What are the symptoms?
There is irritation, swelling and pain in the local area before the formation of blisters. These later become open sores, and are covered with a crust.

Who can get them?
Anyone, but they are uncommon in very young children.

Prevention
- Avoid intimate contact with someone who has the condition.
- Ensure good bowel health.
- Follow a good diet. Refined foods and sugar should be avoided.
- It may be helpful to take a maintenance dose of 250 mg-500 mg L-lysine per day if you have suffered from cold sores before.
- Take daily supplements of vitamin C, vitamin B complex and zinc.

Treatment
- Drink two or three cups of sage tea a day. Make this by steeping two or three sage leaves in a cup of boiling water and adding one tsp of powdered ginger.
- Take a supplement of vitamin A (50,000-100,000 IU a day) in the acute stage. Do not take this dosage for more than a couple of days without medical supervision.
- Take vitamin B3 (500 mg) and B5 (250 mg, twice a day), bioflavonoids (1 g a day), vitamin B complex (50 mg, three times a day), vitamin C (500 mg, twice a day) and zinc (50 mg a day).

- Take L-lysine (500 mg, three times a day), half an hour before meals.
- Take acidophilus daily to recolonise the gut (see p. 31).
- Follow an alkali-forming diet (see p. 185).
- Apply lemon juice, diluted in equal parts with water, to the lesions.
- Rhus toxicodendron and natrum muriaticum taken twice per day each may be helpful. The two remedies should be alternated.
- Under no circumstances try to suppress this condition as it may cause you to have the much more painful shingles or herpes zoster later.

COLIC — see FLATULENCE

COMMON COLD

What is it?
A discharge from the nose, usually colourless. There may be low-grade fever. It is associated with a number of viruses and it may be the prelude to an infection of the windpipe, larynx, sinuses, bronchi or lungs. Some of these conditions are quite serious and should be prevented if possible.

What are the causes?
- The common cold can be caused by a large variety of viruses and it occurs mostly when the vitality is low and the body needs a recharge.
- Low vitamin C levels resulting from any kind of trauma, shock or accident may culminate in a cold.
- Other nutritional deficiencies, especially zinc, may be a factor.
- Overeating, particularly of excessive mucus-forming foods such as dairy products.
- Eating refined foods, particularly sugar and sweets.
- Stress and lack of sleep.
- Poor elimination of waste matter.

What are the symptoms?
A runny nose or blocked nose, heavy head, sneezing and feeling 'off colour' are typical symptoms. A sore throat, loss of voice,

hoarseness, cough and aches and pains are common complications of a cold.

Who can get it?
Anyone, at any time! Colds are highly contagious and places
where large numbers of people are in close proximity to each
other (e.g. churches, schools) provide ideal conditions for 'cold
catching'. You are more likely to catch a cold if you are run
down generally and your resistance is low.

Prevention
- Eat a healthy diet with plenty of vitamin C.
- Do not let yourself become over-tired or over-worked.
- Live the life of a recluse!

Treatment
- Drink a large quantity of fluids, mostly filtered or bottled
  spring water.
- Spend a day or two on raw fruit and vegetables.
- Take daily supplements of vitamin C and zinc.
- Take two or three drops of essential oil of eucalyptus with a
  teaspoonful of honey two or three times per day. Alter-
  natively, add about six drops of eucalyptus oil to a bowl of
  boiling water and inhale the vapour.
- Garlic perles should be taken daily.
- Do not smoke.
- Suggested homeopathic remedies:
  Ferrum phosphoricum: for the very early stages of a cold.
  Aconitum napellus: for frequent sneezing, with a clear,
  warm, watery fluid flowing from the nose. There is fever and
  thirst, but no perspiration. Usually worse in stuffy atmos-
  phere. The remedy should be taken at the first sneeze or
  shiver.
  Allium cepa: for a profuse, watery, acrid discharge. The
  nose and lips are raw and sore and the eyes burn. There are
  bouts of sneezing and the patient feels hot and thirsty, is
  worse in warm room, but better in the fresh air.
  Bryonia alba: the symptoms take a long time to develop.
  The eyes are red and watery. The lips and mouth are dry
  and there is a great thirst for cold water. The patient holds
  head and chest when coughing, and is better when lying
  down or staying still.
  Belladonna atropa: when the cold comes on violently after a
  chill. Little discharge. The nose is sore, red, hot and swollen.
  There is a violent headache with a sore throat, and a great
  thirst.

Gelsemium sempervirens: for a mild cold with a lot of chilliness and shivering. Comes on from change of weather — patient often suffers from summer colds and catarrh. There is a feeling of heaviness in the head, a tearing, tickling cough, but no thirst.

Hepar sulphuris calcareum: discharge is at first colourless but later becomes thick, yellow and offensive. Very sensitive to cold and needs to be completely covered. Peevish and hypersensitive.

Nux vomica: a very good remedy for colds when the nose is alternately blocked and running but stuffed up at night and when in the open air. There is much sneezing and possibly constipation. The patient is thirsty and chilly but better out of doors.

Pulsatilla nigricans: for a persistent cold. Stuffed up at night or in a warm room. Discharge is worse in the evening. Patient prefers a cool room and open windows.

Sambucus nigra: for sniffles or blocked nose in young children.

Teucrium marum verum: chronic catarrh with loss of smell. Useful in hay fever caused by grass pollen.

CONJUNCTIVITIS

What is it?
An inflammation of the eye — specifically of the delicate mucous membrane which covers the surface of the eyeball and the inner eyelid.

What are the causes?
Conjunctivitis can be caused by an infection, an allergy (such as hay fever), or by a foreign body lodging in the eye.

What are the symptoms?
The eye looks red and inflamed. It feels 'gritty' and painful, and there is usually a discharge and watering from the eye.

Who can get it?
Anyone. Those known to be allergic to certain substances, e.g. grass, and those who work with metal and in similar occupations are in greater danger.

Prevention
- Stay away from cut grass, or any similar substances to which you know you are allergic.
- Wear goggles if you work with anything which might throw out splinters.
- Do not share towels, face flannels etc. with anyone who has conjunctivitis.

Treatment
- Take vitamins A, B2, B3, B6 and C.
- Bathe the eyes three times a day with a lotion made by adding one part of homeopathic mother tincture of euphrasia to ten parts of boiled water.
- Dab the eye with a lotion made with one part each of essential oils of lemon and lavender to fifty parts water. The oils may also be massaged around the eyes and face, in which case add five drops of essential oil to one fluid oz of carrier oil.
- Suggested homeopathic remedies:
  Ferrum phosphoricum 6×: five tablets dissolved in hot water, taken four times a day, will usually clear up inflammation and redness of the eye.
  Aconitum napellus: for red eyes which feel hot and gritty. The eyelids are swollen and there is a dislike of light. Profuse watering after exposure to dry, cold wind or bright light.
  Apis mellifica: for swollen eyelids with stinging pain, pus and itching.
  Euphrasia officinalis: for burning and swelling of lids. Eyes water with acrid matter and there is frequent blinking.
  Mercurius corrosivus: Eyelids stick together. There is pus in the eye.
  Pulsatilla nigricans: for thick, profuse, yellow discharge, itching and burning. Lids are sticky and there is a tendency to styes.

CONSTIPATION

What is it?
The infrequent passing of hard stools, often with difficulty and some pain. It is important to note that everyone has a different 'regular' bowel pattern — for some people it may be twice a day, for others it can be every four days or even longer. The pattern

will vary according to the type of food you eat, the amount you eat, whether you take exercise etc. The important factor is whether your normal bowel movements change.

What are the causes?
- The principal cause of constipation is following a diet low in fibre and fluid, but high in refined foods. Common environmental factors, e.g. sharing the same diet, may cause several members of the family to be constipated.
- Other specific dietary causes are excess meat and dairy products, fried food, and tea or coffee. Acid-forming foods (see p. 185) may also cause constipation.
- Lack of water (*not* tea or coffee) may also be a contributory cause.
- Lack of exercise and a sedentary lifestyle.
- Stress — overwork and anxiety are common factors, as is depression.
- Travel (combining stress factors and a different diet from usual).
- Faulty bowel habits: ignoring the 'call'.
- Long-term use of laxatives.
- Liver and gall bladder problems.
- Food allergies.
- Pregnancy — the muscles in the intestine may weaken at this time.
- Certain illnesses, often aggravated by constipation, may also contribute towards causing it: cancer of the colon (constipation may alternate with diarrhoea), diverticulitis, spastic colon, spinal problems, hydrochloric acid deficiency, Hirschprung's disease (an inherited absence of nerve supply to the colon).

What are the symptoms?
Absence of bowel movements at normal times, and/or difficulty in passing stools.

Who can get it?
Some 50-90 per cent of people in Britain and most Western societies suffer from constipation. It is potentially a very dangerous condition, as it can lead to appendicitis, diverticulitis, cancer of the colon, hiatus hernia, piles (haemorrhoids) and anal fissures. In extreme cases it may even cause a stroke.

Prevention
- Eat plenty of roughage in your diet.
- Drink lots of fluids (but cut down on tea and coffee).

- Do not get into the habit of taking laxatives regularly — the bowel will come to depend on them and cease to function normally.
- Chew your food well and don't rush meals.
- Take plenty of exercise.
- Check your posture — a slumped body will not encourage healthy bowel movements. The Alexander Technique (p. 24) is particularly helpful for poor posture.
- Do not ignore the body's natural signals — 'putting off' bowel movements can cause constipation.

Treatment
- Take one tbsp castor oil with orange juice before going to bed. This will normally produce a good bowel movement next morning.
- Eat wholemeal bread, brown rice and unrefined foods, as well as plenty of vegetables and fruit. Eat as much raw food as possible.
- Take at least half an hour's vigorous exercise each day.
- Improve the liver function (see p. 186).
- Learn to cope better with stress.
- Drink *at least* three glasses of water every day and up to two litres if possible.
- Tea, coffee, alcohol, cocoa and cola drinks should be avoided completely until normal bowel movement is restored — thereafter, try to replace them with herbal teas, fruit juice or water.
- Drink the juice of half a lemon in a glass of hot water with a pinch of sea salt and one tsp honey first thing in the morning.
- Take a daily supplement of vitamin C (1-3 g). Magnesium and calcium supplements are also useful.
- The following yoga postures (see pp. 178-181) are particularly helpful for constipation: pavan muktasana, jathara parivartanasana, ardha matsyendrasana, suptra vajrasana, vajrasana and, most important of all, uddiyana bandha.
- Apply firm pressure to the acupoints zhigou (TH 6), zusanli (St 36), hegu (Co 4), zhongwan (Ren 12) and tianshu (St 25). (See p. 165).
- Sitz baths and contrast bathing (see p. 26) can provide relief.
- The essential oils of rosemary, marjoram, hyssop, camomile, camphor and fennel, mixed in a carrier oil and massaged on the abdomen, will help stimulate bowel movement.
- Suggested homeopathic remedies:
Alumina: for dryness of stools, with no urging or movement of bowel for days.

Anacardium: feels as if there is a plug in the anus.

Nux vomica: long history of poor bowel habits often because of laxatives, inattention to regular bowel movements and lack of exercise. Stools are sometimes soft, but there is an unfinished feeling after passing them.

Opium: for round, hard, dry, black stools or for complete inactivity of the bowel.

Plumbum metallicum: a good remedy for chronic constipation, when there is colicky pain and a feeling of urging, but difficulty passing stools.

Silicea: stools are passed with difficulty. When partly expelled they recede again.

Collinsonia canadensis: for obstinate cases of hard stools passed. Piles are often present.

CORNS

What are they?
Small, hard, painful patches of skin on the foot. The core of a corn consists of skin cells packed tightly together.

What are the causes?
Corns are caused by continuous pressure or rubbing on any area of the foot. This is a common effect of ill-fitting, tight shoes.

What are the symptoms?
Corns develop gradually, and before they form there is usually some awareness of discomfort where, for example, a shoe is rubbing a particular area of the foot.

Who can get them?
Women are more prone to developing corns than men because of ill-fitting fashion footwear.

Prevention
- Ensure that your shoes fit properly. If current fashion is dictating that you wear uncomfortable footwear, at least try to alternate between high heels and flat shoes.
- Regular massage of the feet will help keep them healthy.
- Remove rough skin from your feet with a pumice stone or similar, at least twice a week.

Treatment

- Massage the corns with castor oil twice a day, or rub mother tincture of hydrastis in glycerine on to the corn.
- Apply lemon rind to the corn and leave it on during the night. Lemon juice can also be applied.
- Soak the feet in a mixture of warm water and vinegar (one third vinegar to two thirds water).
- Change any tight-fitting or uncomfortable shoes for flatter, more comfortable ones.
- Suggested homeopathic remedies:
  Ferrum picricum: this is the chief remedy for corns. Take the remedy three times per day.
  Silicea: for inflamed corns. It also helps to soften them.
  Ignatia amara: for painful or burning corns.
  Argentum metallicum: for burning corns.
  Lycopodium: for corns with offensive perspiration.
- You may need to visit a chiropodist to have the corns removed if they do not respond to any of the above treatments.

COUGHS

What are they?
A cough is the natural action produced by the surface lining of the upper respiratory tract, in response to any irritation.

What are the causes?
The irritation can be caused by particles of food lodged in the throat, by dust particles or by excess mucus, any of which the respiratory system will try to remove by coughing. Coughs are often the symptoms of infections such as asthma, bronchitis, tonsillitis etc., or of smoking.

What are the symptoms?
There are of course many different types of cough, from the single cough caused by an errant food particle, to the painful spasms of asthma. Coughing is in itself usually a symptom of something else (see 'Causes', above). They are usually worse when lying down at night, or in the morning.

Who can get them?
Anyone.

Prevention

- Follow a healthy diet, low in dairy products and high in vitamins, especially vitamin C.
- Do not smoke.
- At the first sign of a sore throat drink plenty of fluids, including hot lemon and honey drinks at night.

Treatment

- A mucus cleansing diet is important as the first line of treatment, especially with 'wet' coughs. The elimination diet (see p. 187) is very useful for this purpose and should then be followed by a fruit and vegetable diet for a few days. Any fruit except bananas and any vegetable except potatoes or aubergines can be eaten raw or lightly steamed. Do not mix fruit and vegetables in the same meal.
- Take garlic capsules every day.
- Take supplements of vitamins A, B6, B complex and C, and of zinc.
- Drink comfrey tea, made from 1 oz of the dried herb to one pint of boiling water, several times a day.
- Apply a hot compress made with one part cider vinegar to three parts hot water. Soak a towel with this mixture and apply it to the chest. Replace every fifteen minutes until the patient feels better. The cider vinegar mixture may also be used as an inhalant. Place the mixture in a bowl, cover the head and bowl with a large towel and breathe in the vapour through the nose.
- Drink home-made hot lemon and honey if the cough is dry and irritating.
- Suggested homeopathic remedies:
  Antimonium tartaricum: when the cough is brought on by anger.
  Antimonium crudum: for violent coughing which weakens the patient.
  Belladonna atropa: for a barking cough, with three or four bouts of coughing at a time.
  Bryonia: for a dry cough with a stitching pain in the chest, aggravated by going from a warm place to a cold one.
  Calcarea carbonica: for single bouts of coughing.
  Drosera: for a barking type of cough.
  Hepar sulphuris: for a prolonged cough which is worse in the cold.
  Mercurius: when there are two or three bouts of coughing at a time.
  Pulsatilla nigricans: for a cough with yellow expectorate which is better in the open air.

CRAMP

What is it?
An extremely painful spasm of the muscles — usually at the back of the leg — which characteristically lasts for a few minutes. Cramp is not normally serious.

What are the causes?
Cramp is caused by the sudden contraction of muscles, often brought on by salt deficiency (particularly in athletes, or people in hot climates where the body is sweating more than normal). It can also be caused by poor circulation, where the arteries narrow and insufficient blood supplies reach the muscles.

What are the symptoms?
The sudden onset of agonising pain, as described above. The pain lasts for a few minutes only and occurs particularly in the legs, but can also affect the back, neck, sides or face.

Who can get it?
Athletes and those living in hot countries are perhaps more prone to cramp, but most adults have experienced it at some time.

Prevention
- If you are prone to cramps, ensure that you have an adequate salt intake in your diet.
- Follow a low cholesterol diet.
- Ensure that you relax the body as well as exercise it, particularly if you are keen on sports — there are many relaxation tapes available.

Treatment
- Acute cases of cramp should be treated by moving the joint to which the muscles are attached rapidly and vigorously. Sometimes lightly flicking over the muscle with the finger-tips will reduce the cramp.
- For chronic, recurring cramp, apply a small magnet to the area when in bed at night. Keep it in place with a loose bandage.
- Supplements of calcium, magnesium, iron and vitamins C, D, E and B12 are helpful for cramp. People who take a lot of exercise, e.g. athletes, may suffer from cramp because of salt deficiency. Most people, however, take too much salt in

their diet, so try to ensure that you really need it before taking extra.

- A daily dose of kelp (available in tablet form) will often relieve cramp, as it contains most of the nutrients which may be lacking in cases of cramp.
- A very good remedy for cramp is magnesium phosphate — either as a pure substance, or else take three tablets of the 6× potency, dissolved in a little warm water and sipped very slowly.
- Eat plenty of foods rich in magnesium, especially leafy green vegetables, soya beans, nuts (almonds, cashews and Brazil nuts), pumpkin seeds, whole grains and seaweeds (see p. 185 for a fuller list). Buttermilk is also helpful for this condition.

CYSTITIS

What is it?
An acute infection of the bladder.

What are the causes?
Cystitis has several 'trigger factors' — in men, it can be started with an infection of the prostate gland. In women, it can be caused by an allergy, or an infection spread via sexual contact. It is often caused by bacteria from the yeast organism (see 'Thrush', p. 137).

What are the symptoms?
In both sexes, there is a burning pain on passing urine. The sufferer may want to urinate more frequently than usual, but there is no relief on doing so as there is often an accompanying feeling of wanting to pass urine again immediately afterwards. In severe cases there may also be a raised temperature, fever and the possibility of blood mixed with the urine.

Who can get it?
Cystitis is much more common in women — usually young women — than in men.

Prevention
- Eat live natural yoghurt every day, if possible.
- Pay scrupulous attention to personal hygiene.
- Women should always wipe themselves from front to back

with toilet paper, to avoid spreading bacteria from the anus to the vagina.
- Use another form of contraception rather than the pill, if practical, as it depletes essential vitamins from the body.

Treatment
- Drink large quantities of water.
- Avoid acidic foods, such as citrus fruits or anything in vinegar.
- Apply live natural yoghurt to the affected area daily.
- Massage of the acupoints tianshu (St 25) and weizhong (Bl 54) may help (see p. 165).
- Suggested homeopathic remedies:
  Cautharsis: for the typically burning pains on passing urine.
  Staphysagria: for women, when the area is particularly tender.

DANDRUFF

What is it?
Flakes of skin which are shed from the scalp in larger amounts than normal.

What are the causes?
An irregular amount of sebum being made by the sebaceous glands — usually too little sebum is produced, which results in typical white flakes. This may be related to inadequate nutrition and/or stress factors.

What are the symptoms?
The appearance of white flakes in the hair. They are also noticeable on the shoulders when wearing dark clothing. The scalp may feel itchy.

Who can get it?
Anyone.

Prevention
- Do not share combs, hats etc.
- Follow a healthy diet.
- Do not use harsh, cheap shampoos and do not wash the hair every day.

Treatment

- Wash the hair less often than before, with a very mild shampoo.
- Do not rub the scalp with the towel when drying the hair — pat it dry gently.
- Gently massage strong sage tea into the scalp once or twice a week. Wheatgerm or coconut oils are also effective.
- Apply live yoghurt to the hair regularly when washing. Leave for fifteen minutes before washing out.

DEPRESSION — see ANXIETY

DERMATITIS — see ECZEMA

DIARRHOEA

What is it?
The frequent passing of watery or loose stools.

What are the causes?
In chronic (long-standing) cases:
- Overeating (or overfeeding in an infant).
- Poor diet. (Many nutritional deficiencies are associated with causing diarrhoea.)
- Allergies. Cooking in aluminium utensils is a very common cause of allergic diarrhoea, as it reacts strongly with the acid in some foods and can build up in the body.
- Gastritis, colitis or intestinal parasites.
- Stress and emotional problems.
- Anaemia.

In acute cases:
- An infection, often the result of drinking contaminated water.
- Toxins (heavy metals, food pollutants, food poisoning, antibiotics etc.).
- Overeating or too much sugar in the diet.
- Excessive intake of vitamin C.
- Emotional trauma.
- Diarrhoea in an infant may be caused by:
  Poor eating habits of the mother. Cow's milk allergy, if bottle fed. Teething. Infections.

What are the symptoms?
It may be a long-standing problem, or happen suddenly. There may be no other symptoms, or the diarrhoea may be accompanied by pain or discomfort in the abdomen. Sometimes there is considerable flatulence.

Very bad (acute) diarrhoea may be accompanied by scanty urine which is dark in colour, and a dry mouth, weight loss, sunken eyes and a rapid pulse rate.

Who can get it?
Anyone.

Prevention
- Attend to any of the possible causes (see previous page) which may be relevant.
- When travelling, take particular care not to drink the local water unless you know that it is clean, and beware of salads and of fruit which does not need peeling.
- Keep the amount of sugar in your diet as low as possible.
- Use stainless steel cooking utensils rather than aluminium.
- Deal with stress before it becomes a major problem.

Treatment
- The most important treatment for acute diarrhoea is immediate rehydration
  Add two tablespoons of honey, one quarter teaspoon of sea salt and a quarter teaspoon of bicarbonate of soda to one litre of boiled water and mix well. A little fresh lemon or orange juice can be added if possible.
  Give the patient this liquid to sip every five minutes right round the clock, if possible. An adult should drink at least three litres of this mixture in 24 hours, a child about a litre, and less for young children.
- A short fast on water and fruit juice only is recommended, followed by a day or two on very basic foods — boiled brown rice, steamed carrots or live yoghurt are all good. Slippery elm bark should be added to the food or may be taken as a drink.
- Other drinks which are suitable for diarrhoea are camomile, peppermint or raspberry leaf tea.
- A diet of bananas only is also good for diarrhoea. Remove the central cores of the fruit before eating.
- Apply strong stimulation to the acupoints gongsun (Sp 4), zusanli (St 36) and zhongwan (Ren 12) (see p. 165).
- Essential oils of sage, geranium, lavender, peppermint, clove or garlic in a carrier oil, can be massaged into the abdomen.

- Suggested homeopathic remedies:
  Aconitum napellus: for diarrhoea caused by fright or exposure to cold, dry wind.
  Arsenicum album: for severe, burning diarrhoea resulting from tainted food. Vomiting, prostration, restlessness and anxiety. Desire for hot drinks.
  Bryonia: diarrhoea is worse on getting out of bed in the morning. Patient is irritable, and wants to be alone.
  Chamomilla: for diarrhoea associated with teething in infants.
  Colocynthis: for frequent, jelly-like stools with colicky pains. Worse with food or drink.
  Ipecacuanha: for greenish, frothy or slimy stools, with gripping pains around the navel, nausea and vomiting.
  Mercurius corrosivus: for hot, bloody, slimy stools with shreds of mucus. There may be a bloated feeling not relieved by passing stools.
  Nux vomica: diarrhoea from bad dietary habits, often alternating with constipation.
  Rhus toxicodendrum: for diarrhoea with bloody mucus. Tearing pains down legs. Fever and restlessness.

DROWNING — see FIRST AID SECTION

EARACHE AND
EAR PROBLEMS

See also HEARING DIFFICULTIES pp. 103-105.

What are they?
There are several types of earache. Simple earache often accompanies the congestion from a common cold, or boils in the ear canal. An infection of the middle ear may occur when there is an infection behind the ear drum, and may cause considerable pain. This is a common condition in children and may follow tonsillitis, influenza or other episodes of infection. Mastoiditis (see symptoms, overleaf) is a common feature of this condition.

What are the causes?
Earache may be caused by a number of factors, including:

- An accumulation of mucus within the ear, which may be the result of a poor diet.
- Excessive sugar consumption.
- Allergies.
- Wax in the ear.
- Fungus and other infections of the ear, including boils.
- Enlarged adenoids.
- Lowered immunity.
- Infections such as colds, influenza, tonsillitis etc.

What are the symptoms?
Variable, according to the precise condition. Common symptoms of ear disorders include pain in the ear, dizziness, hearing difficulties, noises in the ear and discharge. In mastoiditis the bone underneath the ear is painful and usually there is tenderness and redness over the body area behind the ear. In this case, medical attention is needed.

Who can get them?
Anyone, but earache and ear infections are more common in children. Tinnitus (noises in the ear) is more common in adults.

Prevention
- Take adequate vitamin C.
- Lower your intake of mucus-forming foods, especially dairy products and refined foods.
- Include garlic regularly in your diet.
- For any upper respiratory infection, it is very important to follow an eliminative diet (see p. 187).
- Never insert foreign bodies — cotton buds, keys, etc. — into the ear.
- It is essential to start treatment *immediately* there is the slightest sign of a problem.

Treatment
- If there is stiffness of the neck, severe weakness or loss of alertness accompanying the earache, medical attention should be sought immediately. This is particularly important in the case of young children. If there is no relief within a few hours, medical attention should be obtained.
- Apply firm pressure or circular massage to any of the following acupoints (see p. 165): baihui (Gv 20), ermen (TH 21), tinggong (SI 19), tinghui (GB 2), hegu, (Co 4) and foot-linqi (GB 41). In the case of infection also treat dazhui (Gv 14), quchi (Co 11) and sanyinjiao (Sp 6).
- Two or three drops of warmed honey and garlic oil may be

carefully dropped into the ear last thing at night. Do *not* use crushed garlic. This is particularly helpful if there is a boil in the ear.

- Alternatively, a few drops of mullein essence may be put in the ear three times a day. Mullein has anti-inflammatory properties and eases pain, so this may give sufficient relief that the garlic and honey are not needed.
- Warm salt applications often bring relief. Heat some ordinary salt in a heavy based saucepan and wrap it in a handkerchief. Seal the handkerchief in a sock or stocking to prevent the salt from spilling. Place under the ear when lying in bed.
- Take supplements of vitamins A, B complex, C and zinc, at least until the condition subsides.
- Suggested homeopathic remedies:

Lycopodium clavatum: this is a commonly used remedy in earache.

Ferrum phosphoricum: useful in the first stages of ear inflammation.

Aconitum napellus: when the pain is due to cold.

Belladonna atropa: for throbbing earache, where the pain appears suddenly and is accompanied by a headache. There may be inflammation or boils.

Apis: for stinging pain.

Chamomilla: for pain during teething. The child is irritable and fretful, and better when carried about.

Arnica montana: earache from injury.

Silicea: where there is pus and offensive odour, probably accompanied by boils.

Hepar sulphuris calcareum: the earache is worse in cold weather or when there is the least draught. The pain often starts in the left ear and then moves to the right ear.

Pulsatilla nigricans: indicated when earache follows a cold or develops during a cold. There may be a yellowish or greenish-yellow discharge. A pulsatilla child will be clinging and often screams with pain or weeps. Worse in a warm room, better for open air and less thirsty than normally.

ECZEMA

What is it?
Also known as dermatitis, eczema is an allergic skin condition. There are several different types — contact dermatitis is one of

the most common, occuring when the skin reacts to a substance to which it is sensitive. Eczema usually appears on the hands or face.

What are the causes?

Contact dermatitis is caused when the skin comes into contact with any of a large number of substances to which it is sensitive. Common culprits are: man-made fibres; cosmetics and toiletries; cheap metal jewellery, particularly nickel; soap powders and other cleaning materials. Often the item can be used for a long period before an allergic reaction occurs.

Other types of eczema often go hand-in-hand with asthma, reactions to pollen or other allergies. Children with eczema frequently come from a family with a history of such allergies.

Stress and tension are known to aggravate eczema, although the condition in itself may of course cause stress.

What are the symptoms?

The affected skin often feels itchy and irritated before any visible signs appear. It later becomes red and inflamed, and may turn dry and scaly, or form into blisters, which may open and 'weep'. The degree of inflammation can vary over a period of time.

Who can get it?

Certain people are more predisposed to eczema — those whose families already have a history of allergies and/or those who are themselves allergic/asthmatic.

Prevention

- Wear rubber gloves when washing with detergents etc. (NB. Some people are also allergic to rubber — watch out for symptoms appearing).
- Sort out any stress/tensions, immediate or underlying.
- Include a variety of seeds, nuts and beans, green vegetables and polyunsaturated fats in your diet — all contain essential fatty acids (EFAs), without which the skin can become dry and scaly.
- Choose hypo-allergenic cosmetics, and avoid using hair dyes over a long period of time.
- Avoid nickel-based jewellery and choose clothes with plastic zips, hooks and eyes, etc., if possible.

Treatment

- It cannot be stressed too strongly that skin conditions such as eczema are an indication of toxins in the system. If the eczema is suppressed, the toxins will merely be driven deeper into the body to manifest themselves, sooner or later, as asthma, kidney disease, bronchitis or some other serious problem. For this reason it is better to consult a practitioner rather than to treat the condition yourself. However, the following First Aid measures are helpful:

- Rub the lesions with vitamin E oil or wheatgerm oil. The easiest way to do this is to break open a capsule and rub the contents on to the skin.
- Dandelion is particularly good for eczema — include fresh dandelion leaves in a salad or make dandelion 'tea' or 'coffee' with the dried leaves or root. Add one tsp to a cup of boiling water, leave to infuse and drink three times per day.
- With eczema as with many other conditions, it is very important to improve the general state of health in the body, particularly the bowel, as this is where toxins often collect. Cleanse the bowel by taking castor oil with orange juice at night. This should result in a good bowel movement in the morning — if not, repeat the next night.
- This should be followed by an eliminative diet for a few days (see p. 187).
- Watercress is particularly good for eczema and skin conditions and should be included daily in the diet, if possible.
- A daily zinc supplement is particularly recommended for skin conditions. Other nutrients which may help are vitamins A, B complex, B6, C, D, F, biotin, choline and sulphur.
- Give regular stimulation to the acupoints hegu (Co 4), quchi (Co 11) and sanyinjiao (Sp 6) (see p. 165).

EYE PROBLEMS

What are they?
The eyes are susceptible to a number of self-explanatory conditions, such as night blindness, eye strain, foreign bodies in the eye, blurred vision, watering eyes and twitching. Most are short-term and do not cause lasting damage.

What are the causes?
Obviously, different conditions are related to different causes. However, the main factors are: over-straining the eye muscles (spending long hours doing close work or reading in poor lighting conditions, or under the glare of a VDU screen); and lack of proper nutrition — vitamin A is vital for good eyesight, as are several other vitamins and minerals (see 'Prevention', overleaf).

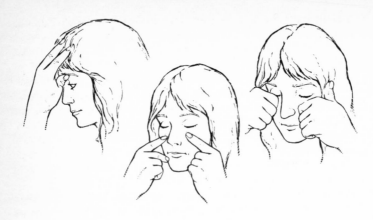

RELIEVING EYE STRAIN

What are the symptoms?
Again, self-explanatory. A headache and/or neck ache often precede eye strain.

Who can get them
Minor eye problems are commonplace, but obviously those whose work involves the close study of text or small items are at greater risk of eye strain. Recent research has also linked VDUs (Visual Display Units) with eye strain among those who use them regularly.

Prevention
- Take the time to practise a few basic eye relaxation exercises regularly (see illustration above, and instructions under 'Treatment').
- Ensure your diet contains adequate supplies of vitamins A, B2, B6 and B12, plus sufficient protein and zinc.
- Always read and do close work in a good light. Look into the distance regularly while doing so to give your eyes a chance to re-focus.
- Wear protective goggles for jobs or hobbies which might involve particles of wood, metal or other irritants getting into the eye.
- Never sit at a VDU screen for more than two hours at a stretch, and ideally less.

Treatment
- Nutrients which are helpful for the eyes are vitamins A, B2, B6, B12, C and E.

- A good bath for sore eyes can be made with a few drops of homeopathic euphrasia (eyebright) in warm water.
- For inflamed eyes, place a slice of cucumber over the eye and leave for ten minutes.
- Essential oils of camomile or lavender are helpful for tired eyes. Add one drop of the oil to a litre of water and soak cotton buds in this lotion. Squeeze out until no longer dripping and apply to the closed eyelids for ten minutes.
- For a stye, sterilize a gold ring with boiling water and rub it gently on the stye. You should also take zinc and multi-vitamin supplements, as styes are a sign of being generally run down.
- For eye strain, massage points around the eye sockets with a circular movement. These are at the inner and outer corners of the eyes and directly above and below the pupils on the bone, as shown in the illustration opposite.
- For black eyes, apply some sort of cold compress or ice pack to the area as soon as possible, to prevent swelling.
- For foreign bodies, stray eyelashes, etc., in the eye, wash out with water or with homeopathic hypericum mother tincture — three drops to 115 ml warm water. If this does not help, put one drop of castor oil into the eye with a dropper.
- Suggested homeopathic remedies:
  Ruta graveolens: for weak vision and eye strain.
  Euphrasia: for infections of the eye.
  Pulsatilla nigricans: for styes.
  Natrum muriaticum: for tired eyes and eye strain, also difficulty in reading in an artificial light.
  Symphytum officinalis: for injury to the eye.
  Arnica montana: for injury and bruising to the eye.

FAINTING

What is it?
Loss of blood to the head and brain which produces dizziness and loss of consciousness.

What are the causes?
Emotional upset, shock, severe pain or exhaustion.

What are the symptoms?
A sudden feeling of weakness in the legs, dizziness and uneasiness. The skin goes cold and pale.

Who can get it?
Traditionally, women are more likely to faint than men, but in reality anyone can faint.

Prevention
Unconsciousness can often be prevented by lying down at the onset of a fainting spell.

Treatment
- Leave the casualty lying flat and bend knees. Do not sit up.
- Vigorously massage the acupoint rhenzong (Gv 26) (see p. 175).
- Give a few drops of the Bach Flowers Rescue Remedy (see p. 17).
- After recovery, sit the patient up and leave comfortable and warm for a while. Sips of cold water may be given if desired.

FEET, ACHING

What is it?
A variety of conditions in which the main problem is painful feet.

What are the causes?
There are numerous contributing factors:
- Weak leg muscles.
- Obesity.
- Ill-fitting shoes.
- Poor circulation.
- Bad posture.
- Too much standing or walking.
- Jogging on a hard surface.
- Constipation.
- Pregnancy.
- Arthritis.
- Walking with the feet turned outwards.
- Lesions of the spine or of the ankle joints.
- Swollen feet.

What are the symptoms?
Symptoms can include: pain in the arches, toes or all over; shifting weight from one foot to the other; inability to get shoes back

on once taken off; 'red-hot' feeling in feet; awareness of general body fatigue caused by aching feet.

Who can get it?
Inevitably, women are more likely to suffer than men because of tight-fitting, high-heeled 'fashion' footwear.

Prevention
- Avoid walking or standing too much, especially when wearing uncomfortable shoes.
- Do not become overweight or constipated.
- If pregnant, take plenty of rest.

Treatment
- If constipated, deal with this immediately (see p. 72).
- Change to more comfortable shoes and walk indoors without shoes when possible.
- Spend some time each day lying with your feet up.
- Check your general posture and if necessary see an osteopath.
- A general foot massage to improve the circulation is often helpful, as is pressure on the acupoint foot-linqi (GB41) (see p. 172).
- Soak the feet in a solution of a few drops of Olbas oil in hot water.
- Try any of the following three easy exercises:
  1. Sit on a chair with your feet off the floor and without shoes on. Stretch your legs out in front of you and circle the feet as vigorously as possible in both directions, then bend the toes forwards and backwards as far as possible.
  2. 'Caterpillar walk'. To do this, simply stand normally, then move forward by bending your toes only.
  3. Walk (indoors) on the tips of your toes.
- Take arnica 3× every two hours and bathe the feet in a hot foot bath to which 1/4 fl. oz arnica O has been added. A hot footbath with Epsom salts is a good alternative, as is contrast bathing — sit with one foot in very hot and the other foot in very cold water.
- Suggested homeopathic remedies:
  Ferrum phosphatum: for burning feet with poor circulation.
  Ruta graveolens: for aching pain and sore tendons.
  Silicea: for cold, sweaty feet and numbness.
  Sulphur: for burning hands and feet. The feet are cold, but burn as if in hot water.
  Sepia: for painful feet during pregnancy.
  Cuprum metallicum: for burning of soles of feet.

Natrum phosphatum: for burning feet at night while menstruating.
Lycopodium: if one foot is hot and the other cold.
Ledum palustre: for difficulty in walking.
Bryonia: worse when walking, better when sitting.
Rhus toxicodendron: worse when sitting, better with movement, and worse in damp cold weather.

- If none of these methods gives relief, consult an osteopath.

FEVER

What is it?
A general term for a condition where the body temperature is raised considerably above the normal level. It is not usually dangerous unless the temperature exceeds 40°C (104°F).

What are the causes?
Usually an infection is the final cause, but other relevant factors may be poor nutrition and the accumulation of toxins due to excessive intake or faulty elimination. In naturopathic terms, a fever is seen as a healing crisis in which the body is trying to recover.

What are the symptoms?
In some cases a fever is short-lived and may only produce mild symptoms or even none at all. Usually there is a feeling of being generally unwell, with a lack of appetite. There may be nausea, vomiting, diarrhoea, headache, sensitivity to light and aches and pains, and in young children there may be convulsions. With persistent or high fever, medical advice should be sought.

Who can get it?
Anyone, but fevers are more common in children.

Prevention
A generally healthy lifestyle with a sensible diet will go a long way towards the prevention of a fever.

Treatment
- Cover the patient completely with bedclothes, leave in a warm room and let them sweat it out.
- Give the patient plenty of fluids — either bottled water only (not tap water) or water and fruit juice (the latter should be

fresh and unsweetened). Fruit may be eaten if the patient wishes — the best fruits are apples, pears, melons, papaya (if available) and grapes. Do not mix more than one fruit at any one time and do not let the patient eat anything else until the fever has subsided.

- Tepid sponging will help to bring down the temperature and is a good treatment for infants and young children.
- Certain essential oils are extremely beneficial for fevers. A mixture of sage, eucalyptus, lavender and thyme applied to the soles of the feet is often effective. Use about 40 small drops in a day: half that amount for an infant.
- Give a homeopathic mixture of aconite, belladonna and camomile. This is known as ABC and can be obtained from a homeopathic pharmacy. Alternatively, kali mur 6× and ferrum phos 6× may be given every two hours for a day or two.

FLATULENCE

What is it?
Abnormal amounts of gas in the digestive tract.

What are the causes?
There are numerous causes of flatulence:
- Poor diet.
- Bad combinations of food, i.e. predominantly carbohydrate foods, such as cereals, with acid fruit.
- Hurried meals or gulping in air whilst eating.
- Allergies.
- Taking liquids with meals (this dilutes the digestive juices).
- Enzyme deficiency.
- Gall bladder disorders.
- Abnormal gut flora.
- Poor posture which cramps the intestines.
- Hiatus hernia (often with pain behind the sternum and blood in the stools).
- Peptic ulcer (often with vomiting, belching and weight loss).

What are the symptoms?
There may be no symptoms other than the passing of wind, which may go upwards or downwards! There may be abdominal distention and discomfort.

Who can get it?
More common in infants (when it is known as colic) and older people, but anyone may suffer from flatulence.

Prevention
- A good diet will help to prevent flatulence.
- Maintain good posture — if you feel you have problems in this area, the Alexander Technique (see p. 24) will help.
- Eat slowly.
- Do not drink with meals.
- Do not mix too many different types of food in one meal.

Treatment
- Do not overeat or hurry your meals.
- Enjoy your food!
- Do not mix too many foods in one meal and take care in the way you combine the foods. Mixing meat and sweet foods or carbohydrate foods in one meal is a common practice which gives rise to fermentation. This produces gas as well as other problems.
- Do not drink with meals.
- Chew each bite of food thoroughly.
- Chewing caraway seeds after a meal may provide some relief.
- Other helpful herbs for flatulence are cloves, coriander, cumin, fennel, ginger, peppermint and thyme. Use them in cooking or chew a clove or a piece of ginger after a meal.
- Take garlic capsules before a meal or cook with plenty of fresh garlic.
- Drink a cup of slippery elm tea three times a day.
- Massage the acupoints hegu (Co 4), zusanli (St 36) and zhongwan (Ren 12) (see pp. 165).
- Yoga postures such as supta vajrasana and pavan muk- tasana (see pp. 178-181) are helpful as they tone up the digestive system generally.

FROZEN SHOULDER

What is it?
A condition where one of the shoulders becomes stiff and pain- ful.

What are the causes?

'Frozen shoulder' may be caused by fibrositis (inflammation of the muscle fibres) or torn fibres, although these are not always the cause.

What are the symptoms?

Stiffness and pain, which often becomes worse at night. The pain is usually particularly bad when the arm is lifted outwards. The condition may worsen for a period of weeks or months, then gradually improve.

Who can get it?

Very often, elderly people who do not move their joints as much as they used to.

Prevention

- Keep the shoulders as mobile as possible, without undue strain from lifting or carrying heavy objects.

Treatment

- Get treatment from an osteopath, chiropractor or acupuncturist at the earliest possible stage. It will be worth it in the long run!
- The tissue salts nat phos (sodium phosphate), kali mur (potassium chloride), mag phos (magnesium phosphate), calc fluor (calcium fluoride) and silica should be taken as a combined remedy.
- You may be able to find some painful points or muscles around the shoulder. Deep massage on these points is often helpful, depending on the true nature of the condition.
- Massage the foot zone reflex point, all around the base of the little toe.
- Massage the shoulder with juniper and garlic oils.
- Homeopathic remedies can also be helpful — sanguinaria is the most commonly used treatment for this condition.

GALLSTONES

What are they?

The formation of concretions, or stones, in the gall bladder. There are three varieties of stones, but most of them contain cholesterol and other ingredients which make up bile.

What are the causes?
- Lack of unsaturated fats.
- Obesity.
- Consumption of rich and refined foods.
- Lack of exercise.
- Negative emotions such as fear, anxiety, anger and hate are potent causes of gallstones since they cause the bile to stop flowing and this encourages stone formation.

What are the symptoms?
Gallstones in themselves do not usually produce symptoms and so many people are unaware of their existence. However, serious complications can arise, such as blockage of the common bile duct, inflammation of the gall bladder, inflammation of the pancreas and cancer of the gall bladder. A common symptom of gall bladder disease is pain in the chest, just below the right shoulder.

Who can get them?
Gallstones occur more often in women and the elderly. Over-weight people are much more likely to suffer from them than people of the correct weight. 'Fat, female and over forty' is the commonly used tag to describe the most likely sufferers. Diabetes, diverticular disease and hiatus hernias are common companions of gallstones.

Prevention
- Eat plenty of fruit, vegetables and unrefined carbohydrate.
- Use poly or mono-unsaturated oils instead of animal fats.
- Take adequate exercise, as this stimulates the gall bladder.
- Reduce your alcohol intake to a minimum and thus keep your liver healthy.
- Take vitamin B complex (brewer's yeast) and vitamin C. Vitamin B helps keep the gall bladder active and vitamin C converts cholesterol into less harmful bile acids. Adequate vitamin A is also important.
- Bear in mind that emotions such as hate, anger and fear are harmful to the liver and gall bladder, so try to avoid situations which provoke them.

Treatment
- Raw, unrefined olive oil is beneficial to gallstones. Use it to cook with, in salad dressings, etc. It can also be taken on its own.
- A fast or mono-diet regime (eating only one type of fruit) is usually helpful.

- Exclude saturated fats from your diet.
- Avoid spicy and fried foods.
- Take supplements of vitamins A, B, C, D, E, K and lecithin. At least 600 mg vitamin E per day is recommended.
- Adopt the principles of prevention outlined on the previous page, especially regular exercise.
- Eliminate or greatly reduce your intake of coffee, tea and alcohol, and do not smoke.
- Essential oils of rosemary, nutmeg, lemon, bergamot, camphor, hyssop and eucalyptus are recommended — massage them, in a carrier oil, into the body.
- L-methionine (500 mg, two or three times a day) is recommended.
- Homeopathic medicines may be helpful, particularly when dealing with colic from gallstones. One of the best remedies for this is magnesium phosphate. Dissolve three tablets in hot water and sip slowly. This solution may also be applied locally.

GENITAL HERPES — see COLD SORES

GERMAN MEASLES

What is it?
A common childhood ailment.

What are the causes?
It is spread by a virus.

What are the symptoms?
German measles normally starts with cold-like symptoms and catarrh. The throat glands may enlarge and become tender. A rash of very small, flat spots will appear in one to two days. Children usually do not suffer very much with German measles, although they are infectious for at least a week, from the start of the catarrh.

Who can get it?
It usually affects very young children, and is a fairly minor disease at this age. However, if pregnant women catch German measles the results can be extremely serious for the foetus, with

a strong likelihood that the baby will be born seriously malformed. It is therefore vital that all women should be vaccinated against rubella (German measles) before they become pregnant. (A blood test will show whether or not the woman is immune, if she is planning to become pregnant and is unsure whether or not she has been vaccinated.)

Prevention
- Vaccination will prevent the virus from attacking.
- If there is an epidemic about, children should be given the homeopathic remedy rubella, three times a day for one day, then once daily for a week.
- It is essential that any child with German measles, or who has been in contact with the disease, is kept at home until the infectious period is over, to avoid any possible contact with pregnant women. Do not allow any women who might be pregnant to visit you during this time.

Treatment
- Give the homeopathic remedies rubella and pulsatilla alternately, two or three times a day.
- Vitamin C supplements daily will help boost the body's natural defences.
- Ensure the patient drinks plenty of water.
- If the spots are irritating, dab them gently with calamine lotion.

GRAZES — see FIRST AID

HAY FEVER

What is it?
An allergic reaction to grasses or pollens, causing irritation to the eyes and nose.

What are the causes?
Hay fever sufferers have a faulty immune system in their bodies which, in effect, makes a mistake about certain otherwise harmless substances — e.g. pollens — by assuming they are harmful, and produces far too much histamine in order to 'fight them off'. This has the effect of causing swelling and excess mucus to form, turning the allergic 'response' into a disease itself.

What are the symptoms?

Watery eyes, streaming nose, sneezing fits, catarrh, sometimes accompanied by coughing. Usually starts in late spring/early summer when the pollen count begins to rise.

Who can get it?

There is a lot of evidence to show that hay fever sufferers either come from a family with a history of allergies, asthma, etc., and/ or have other allergies themselves.

It has also been suggested that those with breathing difficulties — whether caused by smoking, poor posture (thus preventing sufficient oxygen reaching the lungs), or other factors — are predisposed to hay fever.

Constipation should also be considered. If the body is not eliminating toxic waste properly, it will create catarrh in effect to rid itself of the toxins. Catarrh is often linked with hay fever.

Prevention

- Stay away from the offending grasses, plants etc. if at all possible.
- Cut down on dairy products to reduce the likelihood of catarrh (excess mucus) forming.
- Do not allow yourself to become constipated — eat plenty of fibre and drink lots of fluids.
- If your posture is bad, consider the Alexander Technique (see p. 24).

Treatment

- Go on an elimination diet for a few days (see p. 187), then a mucus cleansing diet (see 'Catarrh', p. 64) until the symptoms subside.
- Nutritional supplements which are helpful in allergic conditions are vitamins B5, C, A, E and B complex.
- Red clover helps to control allergies. Make a tea with 1 tsp fresh clover blossoms to one cup of boiling water and steep for ten minutes. Drink three cups per day for a few weeks before the pollen season and if symptoms occur, double the quantity of tea taken.
- Rosehip tea is also useful, as rosehips are a good source of vitamin C.
- Massage the acupoints hegu (Co 4), quchi (Co 11), and yintang (see p. 165).
- Suggested homeopathic remedies:
  Allium cepa 30: a good general remedy for hay fever.
  Arsenicum album: for copious, burning, watery discharge, with chilliness, a craving for warmth, great prostration,

agitation, sneezing and watery eyes.

Kalium bichromicum: for thick, yellow and infected discharge with a sore throat, hoarseness and tough, stringy mucus. Often there is a cough which tends to be worse in the early hours of the morning.

Kalium iodatum: for a thin, burning, hot and acrid discharge with sore throat and puffy eyes. Nose is red and irritated.

Mercuris solubilis: for foul breath and an infected throat. The lymph nodes are often enlarged and tender.

Mixed pollen: potentised pollen is often helpful as a remedy for hay fever, especially late in the season.

Pulsatilla nigricans: for clear, yellow or green discharge. Usually worse in the evening and at night. The sufferer feels chilly, but prefers a well-ventilated room.

Sabadilla: for profuse, watery discharge, sneezing and frontal, sinus type headache.

Teucrium marum verum: for loss of smell. Useful in early, grass-related hay fever.

HEADACHE

What is it?

A pain in or around the head. There are several types:

1 Migraine. This is an excruciating, one-sided pain which often starts in the eye. It may be accompanied by nausea and vomiting, dizziness or visual disturbance.

2 Tension headache. This occurs mainly at the back of the head. It is almost always relieved by lying down.

3 Tumour. This is extremely rare. It comes on slowly and may be suspected if you do not normally suffer from headaches. It is more or less constant, not relieved by anything and usually gets progressively worse. It may be accompanied by mental changes, such as irritability.

4 Allergic headache. This may be similar to a migraine, but usually comes on after a meal.

What are the causes?

Headaches are very common and there are many possible reasons for them:

- Neck problems, including muscle spasm and stiffening of the muscles at the back of the neck.
- Stress, or excessive mental exertion.

- Digestive problems.
- Allergies.
- Low blood sugar.
- Catarrh.
- Anaemia.
- Water retention.
- High blood pressure.
- Menstrual disorders.
- Meningitis.
- Tumours.
- Eye disease and eye strain.
- Arthritis.
- Toxaemia (due to faulty metabolism or to drinking excess tea, coffee or alcohol, some food additives, chemicals added to crops, contraceptive pills and many other drugs).

What are the symptoms?
The pain may be all over the head, or at the top, back or side (see opposite). The headache may be constant, intermittent or recurrent. There may be associated nausea or vomiting.

Who can get it?
Almost anyone can suffer from headaches and most people do. They are much less common in children and more frequent in women.

Prevention
- Eat a sensible diet with few food additives and as much organically grown food as possible.
- Attend to any underlying disorder, especially low blood sugar, allergies, constipation, liver congestion and hormonal imbalance.
- Take adequate exercise in the fresh air.
- Reduce your tea, coffee and alcohol consumption.
- Certain types of food, such as chocolate, yeast extract, red wine, cheese, broad beans and liver sausage contain tyramine which provokes headaches in some people.
- Learn how to relax and cope with stress.

Treatment
- Take short fasts on fruit or vegetable juice.
- At the first sign of a migraine, drink a large amount of water. This will encourage the body to excrete fluid, which may have been contributing to the migraine by causing pressure.
- A cold compress to the back of the head or forehead, with a simultaneous hot foot bath, is often helpful.

- Massage the acupoints hegu (Co4), fengchi (GB20), taiyang, yintang and taichong (Li3) (see p. 165). Any tender points on the head should also be treated with gentle massage.
- The essential oils of lemon, lavender and mint are helpful. Mix them with a carrier oil and massage gently into the forehead and back of the neck.
- Migraine headaches are often related to a food factor. Foods to avoid are cheese, chocolate and red wine. In addition, try to discover if you have any food allergies or intolerances.. The removal of these items from your diet will probably bring immediate relief.
- Good bowel health is very important. Take a tbsp of castor oil with orange juice at night time in order to clear out the system.
- Take vitamins B6 (50 mg a day), B3 (100 mg, three times a day), B12 (10 mg, three times a day), B complex, C (500 mg, two or three times a day). Also recommended are calcium (1 g a day, or 200 mg every hour during acute episodes) and magnesium (500 mg a day, or 150 mg every hour during an acute episode). The vitamin B must be non yeast based if there is an allergy or intolerance to yeast, or a candida infection.
- Relaxation exercises, yoga postures and meditation are recommended to reduce stress.
- Suggested homeopathic remedies:
Aconitum napellus: for a one-sided headache, throbbing over temples or eyes. Feels as if the skull would be forced out of forehead. Better with rest, worse with movement and noise.
Argentum nitricum: head feels much enlarged. Dizziness. Better with pressure.
Aloe socotrena: aches above forehead with heaviness in eyes. Headache from constipation.
Belladonna atropa: for a burning, throbbing headache with violent shooting pains, worse from stooping, jarring, coughing, bending the head backwards or straining when passing stools. Flushed face or dilated pupils.
Bryonia alba: for a bursting, splitting, frontal headache. Better lying down, feels sick and faint on sitting up. Better for pressure and from lying on the affected side. Worse in the morning and from movement. Hot, flushed face, dry and peevish. Likes to be left alone.
Cocculus indicus: for a headache with much retching but little vomiting.
Gelsemium sempervirens: for giddiness and nausea associated with right-sided headache. May have pain at back of

head, which feels like hammering at the base of the brain. Worse for mental effort and heat of the sun.

Glonoine: for a throbbing headache from exposure to sun. Worse from heat, sun, lying down. Better in cool air.

Iris versicolour: for a periodic, throbbing headache over the eye. At first there is blurring of the eyes and at its peak there is vomiting. Affects those who do a lot of mental work.

Nux vomica: for a splitting headache, as if a nail is being driven into the skull. There may be nausea and sour vomiting. May be due to gastric or liver disorders, or getting angry quickly.

Pulsatilla nigricans: a right-sided, periodic headache which descends to the jaw and teeth, particularly after rich food or over-indulgence. Worse for warmth. Patient has no thirst, is moody, peevish and chilly.

Ruta graveolens: for a headache from eye strain. The eyes are red, hot and tired. Possibly accompanied by strained tendons and muscles.

Spigelia marilandica: for a left-sided headache associated with weakness, palpitations and fainting. Normally settles over the left eye. Heart and nervous system are weak. Worse with touch, movement and noise.

HEARING DIFFICULTIES

(See also EARACHE, p. 83)

What are they?
Deterioration of normal hearing abilities in one or both ears, usually over a period of time. Ultimately the sufferer may become completely deaf.

What are the causes?
There are many causes of hearing difficulties. The most likely are: earwax in the ear canal; infections; prolonged exposure to loud noise, e.g. industrial or 'social' (the dangers of high-decibel discos are now becoming well-known); nerve deafness (particularly in older people); fluid in the middle ear; in small children, the possibility of a small object (sweets, beads etc.) having been rammed into the ear by the child.

What are the symptoms?
Loss of hearing, usually gradually, in one or both ears. The sufferer may eventually become totally deaf. There is sometimes

accompanying earache. Intermittent buzzing or ringing noises in the ear are often a first sign of tinnitus (see opposite).

Who can get them?
Deafness is a common 'symptom' of old age, although it is by no means automatic in later years. Sufferers from Ménière's Disease (a degenerative condition of the balance mechanism) suffer many unpleasant symptoms, including deafness in one ear. People who are exposed to continuous or repeated loud noise, e.g. those working with loud drills, are susceptible (although they are usually now issued with ear protectors).

Prevention
- NEVER stick cotton buds, hairgrips or similar objects into the ear — they may damage the eardrum.
- Avoid repeated excessive noise where possible, or use ear protectors.
- If you regularly listen to a 'personal stereo', keep the volume at a reasonable level.

Treatment
- Summer savory is good for hearing problems. Add one oz of the herb to a pint of boiling water. Steep for several minutes and then strain. Drink three cups daily.
- An ointment made by steeping mullein flowers in olive oil for two weeks is good for hearing difficulties. Strain and apply one drop to the ear(s) every day until the condition improves.
- Apply massage to the following acupoints: ermen (TH 21), tinggong (SI 19), tinghui (GB 2), foot linqi (GB 41) and hegu (Co 4) (see p. 165).
- Massage the areas underneath the third, fourth and fifth toes.
- Nicotinic acid (vitamin B3) should be taken for hearing problems. Take 500 mg a day, or twice a day if severe, for several weeks.
- Vitamin E (300 mg, twice a day) should be taken. Lecithin is also helpful in removing cholesterol, which may be a cause of deafness.
- Vitamin C (1 g a day) should be taken. Sometimes a larger dose is required, if there is an infection.
- Suggested homeopathic remedies:
  Phosphorus: in cases where there is headache and tinnitus.
  Phosphoricum acidum: where there is a roaring noise and difficulty in hearing.
  Elaps corallinus: for itching and discharge with chronic deafness.

Calcareum phosphoricum: for deafness with tonsil problems.

Graphites: the patient hears their own voice reverberating inside the ears.

Carbo animalis: where the patient cannot identify the direction of sounds.

Chenopodium anthelminticum: the deafness is specific to low tones.

Salicylicum acidum: useful in simple progressive deafness; often associated with Ménière's disease.

• If all else fails, consult a practitioner about the possibility of osteopathic manipulation.

NOTE

Tinnitus is an unpleasant ailment characterised by ringing or buzzing noises in the ear — which are usually worse at night. The noises can be intermittent at first but become virtually continuous. There is no known cure for this condition — follow the advice under 'Prevention' and 'Treatment' above. Vitamin B complex is thought to be of help.

HEART DISEASE — see ARTERIAL DISEASE

HEART ATTACKS — see FIRST AID SECTION

HERPES ZOSTER — see SHINGLES

HOUSEMAID'S KNEE — see BURSITIS

HICCUPS

What are they?
The term 'hiccups' refers to the involuntary sound produced when an indrawn breath is inhaled and the vocal cord shuts quickly.

What are the causes?
Hiccups occur when the diaphragm (the sheet of strong muscle

which separates the abdomen from the chest) is irritated by the nerves supplying it. A spasmodic contraction of the diaphragm occurs, air is breathed in and the hiccuping noise is heard.

What are the symptoms?
The typical, easily recognizable hiccuping noise, accompanied by a tightness in the throat. Hiccups usually occur in batches, lasting from a few moments to well over an hour in more serious cases.

Who can get them?
Anyone.

Prevention
- Avoid fizzy drinks and foods which you know to be indigestible. Practise deep, regular breathing.

Treatment
- Practise the yoga posture uddiyana bandha (flying contraction) (see p. 180).
- Massage any of the following acupoints: baihui (Gv 20), rhenzong (Gv 26), shanzhong (Ren 17), tiantu (Ren 22), neiguan (P 6) and zusanli (St 36) (see p. 165). Another useful point for treating hiccups is the jianjing point, which is situated just behind the collarbone half way from the centre of the base of the neck and the shoulder. Press downward on this point. It will almost certainly be quite painful, and as it is rather difficult to reach, it is best to get someone else to do it for you. This affects the phrenic nerve and usually stops hiccups.
- A few drops of ginseng in a little water sipped every few minutes is helpful for hiccups.
- When they are caused by indigestion, nux vomica 30 is often helpful.
- If all else fails, see an osteopath for manipulation of the fifth cervical vertebra, or an acupuncturist who will be able to give a more potent treatment.

HIGH BLOOD PRESSURE
(HYPERTENSION)

What is it?
'Blood pressure' is a way of describing the rate at which the

heart pumps the blood around the body. When taking a blood pressure reading, the doctor or practitioner will look at both the figures shown — the top figure gives a measurement when the heart is beating, the bottom figure shows the rate of blood flow between beats.

Normal blood pressure varies from person to person and at different times, but a measurement of over 140 over 90 (shown as $^{140}/_{90}$) is generally taken as being too high. The bottom figure is particularly important as it represents the amount of pressure which has to be sustained by the walls of the arteries. Continuous high pressure may damage the walls and in turn lead to strokes, angina or heart disease.

What are the causes?
There are many contributory factors — not all of which have been proved to cause hypertension, but all of which are known to be linked to it. They include:
- Stress.
- Hereditary factors.
- Pregnancy.
- The contraceptive pill.
- Overweight and a sedentary lifestyle.
- Kidney damage.
- Smoking.

What are the symptoms?
There are no distinctive, recognizable symptoms, so high blood pressure is usually only detected when the blood pressure is measured as part of a health check-up.

Who can get it?
See 'What are the causes?', above. People who may be particularly predisposed to high blood pressure include those who have a family history of the condition; are constantly angry or tense; are overweight and inactive, particularly if their diet is high in salt and saturated fats.

Prevention
- Stay at a healthy weight.
- Do not smoke.
- Do not drink tea, coffee, alcohol or other stimulants.
- Deal with stressful situations rather than let them continue for long periods of time.
- Take regular exercise, of a sort you enjoy.
- If there is a history of hypertension or related illnesses in your family, have your blood pressure checked frequently.

Treatment

- Stop smoking.
- Cut down drastically on salt and animals fats. (Low-sodium alternatives to salt are available if you find food unpalatable without it.)
- Increase the amount of exercise you take, but do not over-exercise if your blood pressure is high.
- Do not allow yourself to become over-stressed. Many of the Bach Flower remedies (see p. 14) are helpful for tension, anger and similar states connected with high blood pressure. Also consider fitting yoga, meditation or relaxation exercises into your daily routine.
- If you feel your general posture is bad, it could be preventing the easy flow of blood around the body. Try the Alexander Technique (see p. 24).
- Take garlic capsules daily to help lower cholesterol levels.
- Hawthorn tea is useful for high blood pressure and tension.
- Massage with essential oils (e.g. lavender in a base of olive oil) will help to relax the body and thus reduce stress levels.

INDIGESTION

What is it?

The uncomfortable, often painful sensations felt in the region of the stomach after eating.

What are the causes?

- Emotional problems, upsets and worry, which deplete the body's nervous energy and weaken the digestive apparatus. They also cause hyperacidity by their chronic influence. An acute upset may result in a lack of hydrochloric acid which will also lead to indigestion.
- Overeating, particularly of fatty and fried foods, or eating too quickly and not chewing the food properly.
- Excessive coffee and tea drinking.
- Unwise combinations of foods. Those which do not combine well are proteins and starches, starches or vegetables and sweet fruit, and proteins with fruit (except for nuts and acid fruit).
- Food additives, especially preservatives, which work against the process of digestion and prevent the breakdown of the food.

- Tobacco smoking.
- Liver and gall bladder problems.
- Obesity.
- Lack of exercise.
- Eating very hot or cold foods.
- Overactivity of the thyroid gland.

What are the symptoms?
Pain and/or discomfort in the stomach area, often with a feeling of bloatedness. Usually occurs after a meal. Heartburn, a 'tight' pain felt higher up behind the breast bone, is a type of indigestion caused by acid coming up from the stomach into the gullet.

Who can get it?
Most people experience indigestion occasionally, but those who regularly eat large, rich meals and/or eat them under stress (e.g. in a hurry, or when in a tense frame of mind) are more prone.

Prevention
(see also 'Treatment' below).
- Avoid foods known to cause problems — for example, pickles cause discomfort for many people.
- Eat properly, chewing your food well, and do not rush meals.
- Follow a healthy, wholefood diet whenever possible.
- Do not drink with meals — drinking dilutes the digestive juices and renders them less effective.
- If suffering from stress symptoms, consider a course of treatment, e.g. meditation, relaxation exercises, etc.

Treatment
- Rest from solid foods for a few days and drink only fresh fruit or vegetable juices.
- Eat slowly and chew all your food thoroughly.
- Eat only when hungry, and do not overeat.
- Do not eat if you are upset, busy or tired. It is better to miss a meal than to eat it when it cannot be digested properly. Replace the meal with a little fresh fruit or fruit juice.
- Do not mix unwise combinations of foods (see 'Causes').
- Do not drink with meals.
- Replace tea and coffee with herb teas. Dandelion 'coffee' is recommended, because it helps to cleanse the liver. Peppermint tea, taken about one hour after a meal, is very effective for indigestion. Add one tsp peppermint leaves to a cup of boiling water and sip slowly.
- Bromelain or papain tablets are helpful. Alternatively, fresh pineapple or papaya, if available, will aid digestion.

- Take regular exercise. Often, a walk before a meal will improve the appetite and aid digestion.
- Apply strong stimulation to the acupoints baihui (Gv 20), neiguan (P 6), zusanli (St 36), sanyinjiao (Sp 6), taichong (Li 3), hegu (Co 4) and zhongwan (Ren 12) (see p. 165).
- Suggested homeopathic remedies:
  Nux vomica: is a good general remedy for indigestion.
  Arsenicum album: when weak, exhausted and fussy, lacking in appetite, chilly and unable to digest anything. Very thirsty.
  Calarea carbonica: when there is a continual sour taste in the mouth. Food is rarely enjoyed and digestion is slow and painful.
  Carbo vegetabilis: for nausea with a sour, acid taste, flatulence and pain at top of abdomen. Worse after eating. The hands and feet are cold.
  Kalium bichromicum: when indigestion is due to drinking too much beer.
  Anacardium: when the problem is relieved by eating, but the symptoms reappear after a few hours.

INSECT STINGS — see FIRST AID SECTION

INFLUENZA

What is it?
'Flu' is an extremely infectious viral disease which spreads rapidly and has severe symptoms — the sufferer usually feels mentally and physically exhausted for at least the duration of the disease.

What are the causes?
- Viruses caught via sneezes, coughs, etc.
- Overeating, especially refined foods and junk food.
- Constipation or an unhealthy bowel, which give rise to toxins.

What are the symptoms?
Prostration, extreme weakness, fever, headache, neuritis-like pains and general muscular aching and loss of appetite. There may be nausea, vomiting and diarrhoea.

Who can get it?
You are more likely to contract influenza if you are run down and there is an epidemic at the time. A person who is infected by the virus but is in good health will not usually contract the disease.

Prevention
There is no guaranteed way to avoid catching influenza — although once you have been infected by one strain, you will be immune to that strain from then on. However, there are many different strains! Obviously those in a good state of health are likely to be more resistant to germs than those in poor health, so do eat well and sensibly, with vitamin and mineral supplements if in doubt.

Treatment
- Cleanse the bowels by taking a tbsp castor oil and orange juice at night. This will help to remove toxins from the body.
- Drink plenty of fluid, either bottled water only (*not* tap water), or a mixture of water and fruit juice. The latter should be fresh and unsweetened. Whole fruits may be eaten if wished. The best choices are apples, pears, melons, or grapes. The fruits should not be mixed at any one time.
- Homeopathic cadmium sulphate CM and cinnamon 200 should be alternated every two hours throughout the day for a day or two until the symptoms start to subside.
- Massage the acupoints quchi (Co 11), hegu (Co 4), dazhui (Gv 14), zusanli (St 36) and sanyinjiao (Sp 6) (see p. 165).

INSOMNIA

What is it?
Sleep problems.

What are the causes?
- Anxiety, tension and other forms of emotional stress. Typically this leads to difficulty getting off to sleep.
- Depression. This often leads to wakefulness, especially early in the morning.
- Physical tension, muscular aches and tightness, liver and gall bladder problems. These almost invariably lead to waking up in the very early hours of the morning.
- Indigestion — this usually leads to wakefulness an hour or two after going to sleep.

- Coffee, tea, cocoa and other stimulants which lead to difficulties in getting to sleep.
- Toxaemia. This may prevent you getting to sleep or cause wakefulness during the night.
- Pain, which usually prevents the person from getting to sleep and causes wakefulness during the night as well.
- Overwork or working just before going to bed, or working and sleeping in the same room.
- An uncomfortable bed, the room too hot or too cold, lack of air or too much noise.
- Vitamin B deficiency, thyroid disorders, smoking and food additives may also contribute.

What are the symptoms?
There are three types of insomnia: inability to get off to sleep; wakefulness during the night; early waking. Concurrent problems are waking up tired, feeling irritable and a lack of concentration.

Who can get it?
Anyone, apart from perhaps newborn babies, but it is much more common in older people. In children, it is usually associated with some psychological disturbance.

Prevention
Not really applicable. Attend to any of the causes above that are relevant to you.

Treatment
- Try to find the basic cause of the insomnia, if possible, and treat it accordingly.
- Treat any underlying stress or anxiety.
- Ensure that the bedroom is well ventilated and neither too hot nor too cold. Also, don't work in your bedroom: keep it for sleeping!
- Take enough physical exercise during the day that your body is tired at night.
- Some people are kept awake by certain types of films, books or radio programmes as well as by arguments and emotional upsets. If this is true for you, try to keep the later part of the evening free for reading suitable literature or listening to restful music.
- Ensure that your bed is comfortable. The mattress should be firm without being hard and should not sag. The pillow (one is better than two) should be at the correct height for you.

- Do NOT take sleeping tablets, because most of them deprive you of one of the essential phases of sleep. If you have just stopped taking these tablets don't be surprised if your sleep pattern is abnormal for some time, while the body makes up for the lack of what is known as REM (rapid eye movement) sleep. This causes wakefulness. Herbal sleeping tablets, however, are non-addictive and do not interfere with sleep, so may be taken safely.
- Take L-tryptophan (1 g during the day and ½ g at bedtime). Always take it at least half an hour before a meal. The bedtime dose should be taken well after your evening meal, if possible.
- Take calcium supplements (1,000-1,500 mg a day) and magnesium (500 mg a day).
- Other nutritional supplements which may be helpful are Vitamin B complex, vitamin B6 (100 mg, twice a day), vitamin B5 (250 mg a day), zinc (15 mg, twice a day) and manganese (5 mg a day).
- A tepid bath before going to bed is recommended for insomnia. The essential oils of basil, camomile, marjoram, sandalwood or lavender can be added to the bath water or massaged (in a carrier oil) into the body.
- Do not eat a heavy meal late at night. If you have digestive problems, eat only a light dinner and make up for it at lunchtime.
- Hot footbaths are useful as they help to drain the blood from the head and make sleep easier.
- Massage the acupoints shenmen (H 7), hegu (Co 4), baihui (Gv 20), shishencong, neiguan (P 6), shenmen (H 7), anmian 1 and anmian 2 (see p. 165).
- Suggested homoepathic remedies:
  Chamomilla: for insomnia caused by pain or cramps with increased irritability, and for teething children.
  China officinalis: for sleeplessness caused by crowding ideas into the mind or after excessive tea or coffee drinking.
  Cocculus indicus: if you are exhausted and over-tired, especially after a long journey.
  Coffea cruda: for sleeplessness after too much excitement.
  Lachesis: if you feel sleepy, but cannot 'nod off'. For restless sleep with many dreams.
  Lycopodium clavatum: for those whose mind is frequently overactive in the late evening but who can sleep soundly in the morning.

JOINTS, PAINFUL — see BURSITIS

LARYNGITIS — see SORE THROAT

LEUCODERMA

What is it?
Depigmentation of the skin, occurring in patches.

What are the causes?
Usually unknown, but secondary leucoderma may follow burns, scars and skin infections. There may be an endocrine disturbance. It may also be caused by smallpox vaccination.

What are the symptoms?
Light areas of skin, which contrast markedly with the surrounding skin in darker-skinned people.

Who can get it?
It seems to be more common in females.

Prevention
Unfortunately, since the precise causes of leucoderma are not known, no preventative steps can be recommended.

Treatment
- Vitamin A and zinc supplements are recommended.
- Treating the lesions with acupuncture often shows good results.
- Suggested homeopathic remedies:
  Sepia: the main remedy for this condition. Most useful in young people.
  Arsenicum album: for dry, rough and scaly skin. The patient feels worse in the cold.
  Arsenicum sulfuratum falavum: when the skin is chaffed around the genitals.
  Selenium: for itching around the ankles and dry, scaly eruptions on palms.
  Manganum aceticum: for cracks in the bends of the elbows and itching.
- It is most important to protect the affected areas of skin from the sun to prevent burning.

LEUCORRHOEA

What is it?
A vaginal discharge.

What are the causes?
- A disturbed acid/alkaline balance in the body, mainly caused by overconsumption of refined foods, junk foods, meat, alcohol, tea and coffee.
- Incorrect balance of the flora in the gut, caused by poor diet and/or taking antibiotics.
- The contraceptive pill which changes acid/alkaline balance and creates a vitamin B6 deficiency.
- Tight-fitting, synthetic underwear (e.g. nylon) which prevents proper breathing of the tissues and the evaporation of perspiration.
- Poor hygiene, or sexual contact with a man with poor hygiene habits.
- Diabetes.
- Many drugs, especially corticosteroids.
- Spinal lesions or imbalance. This can lead to impaired circulation in the vagina and pelvic organs.
- Stress. This upsets the normal hormonal balance and also decreases the blood supply to the vagina.

What are the symptoms?
The vaginal discharge is usually white in colour. There may be other symptoms, such as itching and pain.

Who can get it?
It may occur in any female, but in young girls it may be a hormonal problem.

Prevention
- Take a good, predominantly vegetarian diet, without refined carbohydrates.
- Learn to deal with stress properly.
- Good vaginal hygiene does not necessarily mean frequent douching — washing the area once a day is quite adequate. After visiting the lavatory, always wipe yourself from the front to the back, to avoid spreading any infection from the anus.
- Wear loose-fitting underwear made of cotton.
- Do not take antibiotics, as they seriously interfere with the

balance of micro-organisms in the gut, which can lead to leucorrhoea and many other problems.

Treatment
- Take the following supplements: vitamin A (25,000 IU, two or three times a day), vitamin B complex (100 mg, twice a day), vitamin B6 (50 mg, twice a day), vitamin C (three to five a day), vitamin E (400 mg a day), garlic (two capsules, three times a day), Super Dophilus tablets, three times a day.
- Suggested homeopathic remedies:
  Alumina: for a thin, white, irritating and burning discharge before or after menstruating.
  Borax: when the discharge is like the white of an egg, feels hot and usually occurs in mid cycle.
  Calcarea carb: for a persistent yellow, milky discharge. The hands and feet are cold and damp. Useful for young adolescent girls and for overweight, 'flabby' types.
  Kreosotum: yellow, watery, acrid discharge which smells like fresh grain. Worse after a period. Redness, itching and burning of the vulval area.
  Platinum muriaticum: for a watery discharge with much itching, often accompanied by depression and constipation.

LICE

What are they?
Lice are tiny parasitic insects which live by sucking blood from the skin. The most common type are head lice, usually found on schoolchildren.

What are the causes?
Lice like to live in warm conditions where they are undisturbed; that is why an epidemic of head lice usually starts with children who are neglected and who live in unhygienic conditions. As lice are very infectious, they can easily spread to the rest of the children in one class and, thus, to the whole school.

What are the symptoms?
Frequent itching and scratching of affected area. By using a fine comb, it is often possible to see the egg cases ('nits'), clinging to the base of the hairs next to the scalp. If the child is badly affected, listlessness and lethargy may set in.

Who can get them?

Head lice are most commonly found in schoolchildren or younger children who attend nursery schools or playgroups. They are highly infectious.

Body lice are rare nowadays except in tramps and those living in insanitary conditions, although pubic lice (sometimes known as 'crabs') can be spread via sexual contact.

Prevention

- Strongly discourage children from sharing hats, scarves etc.
- Comb the child's hair frequently with a fine-toothed comb and wash regularly.
- The risk of pubic lice will obviously be reduced if the number of sexual partners is kept to a minimum.

Treatment (for head lice)

- Wash the hair with cider vinegar. Leave for half an hour and then rinse. Repeat several times a day until the lice have all been removed.
- Alternatively, wash the hair with sabadilla (cevadilla seed) lotion, prepared by adding two parts of mother tincture to twenty of water. This treatment should be repeated daily for as long as necessary.
- Suggested homeopathic remedies:
  Ledum palustre: for itching and irritation.
  Tuberculinum bovinum 30: often helpful in chronic cases of infestation.
  Staphysagria: for severe itching and a constantly irritating scalp. This provokes frequent scratching and infection. The infection produces a dirty-looking, oozing discharge and the patient is annoyed if the head is examined.
  Natrum muriaticum: useful when there is a greasy scalp and dandruff. There are often irritating eruptions around the hairline.

MEASLES

What is it?

An acute contagious viral disease, usually affecting young children.

What are the causes?

The immediate cause is a virus. Predisposing causes are lack of or poor nutrition, lymphatic congestion, lack of sufficient fresh air, and suppression of other conditions in the child or the parent.

What are the symptoms?
Measles start with fever, runny nose, possibly a frontal headache, catarrh and aches and pains. Later a rash appears (dark red, blotchy eruptions start around the ears and spread over whole body). The eyes are sore and red and there is an aversion to light. The child feels miserable and often has a barking cough. Complications of bronchitis and pneumonia may arise if the case is not treated properly.

Who can get it?
Although adults can catch measles, it is far more common in children. As it is carried by a virus, schools, playgroups, etc. are ideal breeding grounds for the disease.

Prevention
- A sound diet is important.
- Good hygiene.
- Adequate vitamin C.
- When there is an epidemic, give homeopathic morbillinum three times on the first day and weekly thereafter.

Treatment
- See treatment for fever (p. 92).
- A fruit juice fast is essential.
- Give large amounts of vitamin C (up to 30 g on the first day and smaller doses thereafter).
- Apply essential oils of thyme, lavender or eucalyptus, either directly onto the soles of the feet (about 20 drops of combined oils in 24 hours) or dissolved in a carrier oil and massaged into the chest and back.
- Suggested homeopathic remedies:
  Morbillinum: this can be used at any stage of the disease.
  Aconitum napellus: for high fever, chilliness, dry cough, frequent sneezing, pain in the chest and restlessness.
  Bryonia alba: when the child is very thirsty and has a dry, hacking cough.
  Euphrasia officinalis: for streaming, painful nose and eyes and dislike of light.
  Ferrum phosphoricum: when the skin is hot and the throat painful and swollen, but the child is intolerant of heat and of cold draughts.
  Belladonna atropa: the face and eyes are flushed and there

is high fever and severe headache. The child feels drowsy but does not go to sleep.

Arsenicum iodatum: for profuse night sweating. Child unable to move when fever at its peak.

MENSTRUATION — see PREMENSTRUAL TENSION

MOUTH ULCERS

What are they?
Small, raw sores on the inside of the mouth, where the skin is thin and can be easily damaged.

What are the causes?
Mouth ulcers are generally thought of as a sign of being 'run down' and indeed they can be a side effect of certain illnesses, e.g. anorexia nervosa. They can also be a result of stress, either directly or indirectly (i.e. by constantly biting the inside of the mouth, as a nervous habit). A deficiency of vitamin B2 is often associated with mouth ulcers.

What are the symptoms?
Sufferers are usually well aware of mouth ulcers as they are often self-inflicted (e.g. through biting the inside of the mouth or wearing ill-fitting dentures). The ulcers are normally painful and may bleed.

Who can get them?
Those who are run down, follow a poor diet and are lacking in essential nutrients, or who have developed a nervous habit of biting the inside of the mouth, are more prone to mouth ulcers, but they are quite common in the population as a whole.

Prevention
Be particularly careful to eat well — a varied, wholefood diet rich in vitamin B2 (found in yeast, vegetables, grains, eggs and fish) — see p. 183.

Treatment
• Rub the ulcer with a lotion made from six drops of oil of

coltsfoot, three drops of oil of myrrh and ½ tsp honey.
- A few days on an elimination diet (see p. 187) is helpful.
- Reduce your sugar intake.
- Stop smoking if you still do.
- Take garlic, fresh or in capsules, regularly.
- Tissue salts are effective for mouth ulcers. Usually, a combination of sodium phosphate (nat phos) and potassium phosphate (kali phos) or potassium chloride (kali mur), magnesium phosphate (mag phos) and silica will suffice.

    If there is also a liver disorder or water retention, then sodium sulphate (nat sulph) should be used instead of sodium phosphate.

MUMPS

What is it?
A swelling of glands (mainly the salivary glands) with a fever.

What are the causes?
A virus, coupled with reduced immunity.

What are the symptoms?
There may be some low grade fever and sore throat for a day or two, followed by swelling of the salivary glands in the cheeks which produces the characteristic appearance of mumps. The swelling is often worse on one side and may last from about four to ten days. There may be some discomfort in the area, which is made worse by eating or drinking acidic or sour substances. There may also be headache, fatigue and loss of appetite. In adult males, there may also be swelling of one or both testes.

Who can get it?
Mostly children between the ages of five and fifteen, but it can affect older people. Mumps are rare, however after forty.

Prevention
- Avoid close contact with anyone who has mumps.
- Large amounts of vitamin C can increase immunity.
- Two or three doses of homeopathic parotidinum 30 can be given during an epidemic.

Treatment
- Drink only water and fruit or vegetable juice for a day or

two. A hot drink of Vecon (vegetable bouillon) may also be given.

- Give 3 g of vitamin C a day while the condition lasts.
- Massage the acupoints hegu (Co 4), zusanli (St 36), dazhui (Gv14) and quchi (Co 11) (see p. 165) to help improve the immune system.
- Gently rub the essential oils of lavender and sage, in a carrier oil, to the top half of the body.
- Suggested homeopathic remedies:
  Phytolacca: for most cases of mumps.
  Belladonna atropa: when there is redness and swelling especially on the right side of the face.
  Rhus toxicodendrum: if there are dark red swellings, worse on the left side and 'sticking' pains when swallowing.
  Mercurius: if there is pale swelling, with stiff jaws and considerable pain and salivation.
  Pulsatilla nigricans: for swelling of the testicles.

NAPPY RASH

What is it?
An unsightly red rash appearing on a baby's bottom.

What are the causes?
The rash is caused when urine on the nappy comes into contact with the baby's skin — not immediately, but after some time, the bacteria naturally present in the skin reacts with the urine to produce ammonia, which attacks the skin.

It may also be caused by an infection, and is worsened if the baby has loose bowel movements, as the bacteria from the faeces combine with the ammonia to create further irritation.

What are the symptoms?
The appearance of red spots and rough skin all round the baby's bottom. The rash is obviously painful and may worsen, with the skin breaking and 'weeping'.

Who can get it?
Almost all babies have nappy rash at some time.

Prevention
- Keep the baby clean and dry, with frequent nappy changes.
- If breastfeeding, cut down on spicy and acidic foods.

- Do not put plastic pants on the baby — they create warm, moist conditions in which bacteria rapidly grow.
- If using fabric nappies, wash them thoroughly (boil if possible), rinse well and make sure they are completely dry before using them.

Treatment
- Boil fabric nappies, if used.
- Let the child go without a nappy, whenever possible.
- Dry the skin very well after cleaning.
- Smear vitamin E cream over the baby's bottom.
- Do not use plastic pants on the child at all.
- Suggested homeopathic remedies:
  Rhus toxicodendrum: for severe rashes with blisters.
  Sulphur: for rashes which appear worse after the baby has been in contact with heat or warm water.

NOSEBLEEDS

What are they?
A common occurrence, with a sudden showing of blood from the nostrils. It is usually of little consequence, but may occasionally indicate a serious disorder.

What are the causes?
Common causes are:
- A sudden blow to the nose.
- Violent exercise.
- A foreign body in the nose.
- High blood pressure — the bleeding is often accompanied by dizziness and a headache.
- Vitamin C or vitamin K deficiency — there may be blood in the urine and bleeding from the gums and vagina as well as from the nose.

What are the symptoms?
The sudden appearance of blood from the nostrils — which can be anything from a copious flow to a few drops on a handkerchief.

Who can get them?
Nosebleeds can occur at any time, but if they happen regularly,

they may be a symptom of other conditions (see 'What are the causes?', opposite) and should be treated accordingly.

Prevention
- Don't put foreign bodies into the nose.
- Deal with any of the problems under 'Causes' that might exist.

Treatment
- Sit the patient down and make sure their head is bent forward.
- Loosen any tight clothing around the neck and chest.
  Put a bowl in front of the patient.
  Ask the patient to breathe slowly through the mouth and at the same time lightly pinch the soft parts of the nose together.
- With those suffering from high blood pressure, it is unwise to stem the bleeding too quickly because it may be a form of safety valve. Allow the bleeding to continue for at least ten minutes before taking remedial action.
- The patient should avoid swallowing the blood.
- Apply a cold pack (e.g. ice cubes wrapped in a clean handkerchief) to the bridge of the nose.
- Do not let the patient blow the nose for some time after the nosebleed has stopped.
- Suggested homeopathic remedies:
  Phosphorus: for all forms of bleeding.
  Ferrum phosphoricum: when there is a catarrhal condition of the nose.
  Ammonium carbonate: when the nose bleeds after washing the face or eating.
  Rhus toxicodendrum: for nosebleeds after strenuous exercise.
  Lachesis: for nosebleeds in hot weather.

PILES (HAEMORRHOIDS)

What are they?
A painful condition where the veins in the rectum become swollen and twisted, and tend to prolapse. They may occur inside or outside the anus — when outside, the protrusions may be easily seen or felt.

What are the causes?

The principal cause seems to be a low-fibre diet which results in constipation and hard, sticky stools. These damage and dislodge the delicate lining of the rectum and the small veins which are situated around the anus.

Other causes:
- Overeating.
- Repeated use of laxatives.
- Vitamin deficiency, especially vitamin B6.
- High blood pressure.
- Heart problems, liver disorders or pregnancy.

What are the symptoms?

The symptoms are pain, itching and often a sense of 'fullness' round the back passage. The sufferers are usually constipated and the condition may be aggravated by passing hard stools. Internal piles often bleed, but there is no need for alarm if the blood is a bright red colour.

Who can get them?

Those prone to constipation are more likely to suffer from piles. However, it is completely untrue that piles can be caused by sitting on radiators!

Prevention

- Follow a high-fibre diet to prevent constipation.
- Take regular exercise to keep the circulation healthy.

Treatment

- Drink plenty of water or fruit juice.
- Apply witch-hazel, in an ointment or as suppositories.
- Strong stimulation to the acupoint baihui (Gv 20) (see p. 175) often gives relief. Another acupoint which may help is sanyinjiao (Sp 6) (see p. 168).
- Suggested homeopathic remedies:
  Mariaticum acidum: when the haemorrhoids are very painful to the slightest touch and worse in damp weather.
  Nitricum acidum: when there is pain after passing stools and considerable bleeding.
  Sulphur: for redness around the anus with itching.
  Pulsatilla nigricans: useful in pregnancy.
  Nux vomica: particularly for people with a sedentary lifestyle. There may be itching and a frequent urge to pass stools, which continues even after passing a motion.

Very often nux vomica at night time and sulphur in the morning will cure the problem.

PREMENSTRUAL TENSION (PMT)

What is it?
A variety of symptoms occurring shortly before menstruation. These include swelling of the abdomen or ankles, pain in the lower back, swollen breasts, cramps, headache, insomnia, lethargy, depression and even aggressiveness.

What are the causes?
- Low blood sugar and nutritional deficiencies are often connected to PMT.
- Zinc, magnesium, and vitamin B deficiencies are very common in PMT. Vitamin F (essential fatty acid) may also be deficient.
- Excess tea, coffee, alcohol, chocolate, cocoa, and cola drinks.
- Osteopaths often find structural problems of the lower back, which cramp the uterus, in PMT sufferers.
- Congestion of the liver.
- Heavy metal toxicity.
- Water retention.

What are the symptoms?
A wide variety of unpleasant symptoms may occur — most sufferers have many, if not all, together. Most common are: swelling of the breasts, abdomen and ankles; pain in the lower back and abdomen; cramps; headaches; tension around the neck and shoulders; irritability and/or depression; mood swings; weight gain because of fluid retention. Most of the symptoms start around 8-10 days before the menstrual period begins.

Who can get it?
Obviously, only women. However, some women go through life with few, or no, symptoms of PMT; and those who are prone are in general perfectly healthy otherwise. PMT is most common in women over 30.

Prevention
As there is no easily identifiable cause for PMT, prevention cannot be guaranteed. General advice, however, includes:

- Drink plenty of fluid, but avoid drinks which contain caffeine (coffee, tea and cola drinks).
- Deal with stress/tension as it appears.
- Take plenty of exercise.

Treatment

- Take supplements of magnesium (500 mg a day), oil of evening primrose and vitamin B6 (100-200 mg a day), while the symptoms persist (*not* all month).
- It helps to stop taking any drink containing caffeine such as tea and coffee. Replace these with water, fruit juice or herb tea.
- With all menstrual troubles make sure the liver is in good condition and draining well — have a check-up if in doubt. If you are angry or frustrated, there may be trouble in the liver.
- Massage the acupoints sanyinjiao (Sp 6), yaoyangkuan (Gv 3), xinjiang (Li 2) and taichong (Li 3) (see p. 165).
- Bach Flower remedies which are useful for PMT are agrimony, cherry plum, gorse, olive, mustard, sweet chestnut and vervain.
- Suggested homeopathic remedies:
Belladonna atropa: for pain the day before the flow starts. The intestines feel as if they are being forced through the vagina. The face is red and throbbing.
Chamomilla: for dirty looking clots of blood, labour-like pains and increased frequency of passing urine.
Gelsemium sempervirens: for sharp spasms in the lower abdomen and back.
Magnesium phosphoricum: for colicky spasms in the pelvis, which are better after hot applications or massage.
Pulsatilla nigricans: for cutting and tearing pains in lower abdomen, with loss of appetite and diarrhoea during periods, blood clots.
Sulphur: for irregular periods which are accompanied by a burning pain.

PROSTATE PROBLEMS

What are they?

The most common problem is enlargement of the prostate gland which occurs in a very large proportion of men over the age of 60. The onset is usually slow and the condition can be serious, as the prostate surrounds the urethra. An enlarged urethra may constrict and so impair or even prevent the flow of urine. Adddtionally the condition sometimes leads to premature ejaculation and impotence.

The prostate may also become infected — this usually causes a general feeling of ill-health. There are problems passing water, and, frequently, back pain.

Another fairly common problem of the prostate is cancer — this is rare in men under 60. The first symptoms may be severe back pain, but there may also be problems passing water.

What are the causes?

The cause of prostate problems is often said to be ageing, but it must be stressed that it is not a normal part of the ageing process. The most important cause of prostate problems is usually nutritional deficiency, particularly zinc deficiency. This is prevalent in modern society and affects men much more than women. Other possible contributory factors may include lack of exercise and a sedentary occupation, constipation, infections and lymphatic congestion.

What are the symptoms?

- Difficulty in starting to pass urine
- Increased frequency of urination and dribbling of urine from the penis afterwards.
- Sleep may be interrupted.

Who can get them?

Prostate problems are rare in men under 60.

Prevention

- Take zinc supplements regularly, especially if you are over 40.
- Massage the area between the anus and the genitalia regularly.
- Regular exercise. This helps to keep the lymph moving well. The yoga postures jathara parivartanasana and dhanarasana (see pp. 180-181) are also particularly helpful for this. Ensure that there is ample fibre in your diet and avoid becoming constipated.

Treatment

- Take a daily (10 mg) supplement of zinc. If you have suffered from prostate problems before, or have serious symptoms at present, increase the dose to 50 mg a day and take a daily supplement of magnesium. The following daily supplements are also recommended: vitamin A (25,000 IU), vitamin B6 (100-200 mg), vitamin B complex, vitamin C (1 g or more), vitamin E (500 mg), vitamin F.

- Pumpkin seeds are very beneficial for the prostate, because of their high zinc content, as are sunflower seeds or sunflower seed oil. Sunflower seeds can be ground and blended with water to make a nutritious and pleasant alternative to coffee or tea, both of which have an adverse effect on the prostate.
- Contrast bathing in alternate hot and cold water, or sitz baths are recommended (see p. 25).
- Have an osteopath check your spine for possible lesions. Yoga postures which are especially beneficial for this condition are especially ardha matsyendrasana, dhanarasana and bhujangasana (see pp. 179, 181).
- An effective exercise to strengthen the prostate and surrounding area is periodically to tighten the peri-anal muscles. This is done by 'pulling in' as if trying to prevent urination or passing stools. Hold the position for as long as is comfortable and then relax. Repeat several times in a session and repeat the sessions several times per day.

ROAD ACCIDENTS — see FIRST AID SECTION

SHINGLES

What is it?
Shingles (herpes zoster) is a skin condition, thought to be related to the chickenpox virus.

What are the causes?
Shingles is caused by a virus which may be encouraged by poor nutrition.

What are the symptoms?
Blister-like sores on the skin sited along the course of a nerve. The rash usually disappears after a week or so but the burning pain continues, often for quite some time. The usual areas of infection are the chest, trunk and face.

Who can get it?
It most often occurs in people over the age of 40 and is less

common in those who have previously had chickenpox.

Prevention
See notes under 'Cold sores' — they are another form of the herpes virus.

Treatment
- Rub the lesions gently with vitamin E oil.
- Take a supplement of L-lysine (500 mg, three or four times a day, half an hour before meals).
- It is important to free the body from toxins which may stop the body from healing itself. Take a tbsp. of castor oil with orange juice before going to bed. Follow this with daily supplements of acidophilus, as tablets or in certain types of live yoghurt.
- In severe cases, follow a fruit juice fast for two days.
- Drink nettle tea or sage tea in place of ordinary tea or coffee.
- Take 25 mg of vitamin B12, three times a day, with meals.
- Large doses of the vitamins B complex, B3, B5, B6, C and bioflavonoids should be taken daily.
- The essential oils of lemon, geranium, camomile, bergamot and lavender will give some relief. They can either be mixed and massaged into the soles of the feet or dabbed into the lesions.
- Suggested homeopathic remedies:
  Urtica urens: for swelling and large blisters.
  Rhus toxicodendron: for redness and itching. The patient is better for warmth and movement, but worse in bed.
  Apis mellifica: for burning and stinging pain with redness and swelling. The patient is restless and less thirsty than usual.
  Ranunculus bulbosus: when the lesions are black, with intense itching and the patient is worse in the open air.
- Acupuncture often gives relief to shingles sufferers.

SLEEP DISORDERS — see INSOMNIA

SMOKING — RELATED CONDITIONS

What are they?
Tobacco smoking is not an illness in itself, of course, but it is an extremely dangerous addiction — the list of nicotine-related

illnesses is long and growing. For example: nicotine affects the arteries in the eyes, so can cause defective eyesight; gives bad breath and imparts an unpleasant smell of stale smoke to the clothes and hair; causes a bad cough and often bronchitis; makes the smoker more susceptible to infections, as it depletes the vitamins in the body; causes diarrhoea and palpitations; has a direct link to angina and heart attacks; is a known factor in cancer of the lungs, bowel, mouth and throat; can cause smaller and therefore unhealthier babies to be born. On average, non-smokers live 10 to 15 years longer than smokers.

What are the causes?
Nearly all people who smoke began as teenagers or sometimes even as children. However, the main problem is that once started, smoking is very difficult to give up because nicotine is an addictive substance. Cigarettes are still widely advertised in women's magazines, sports sponsoring, etc., and are invariably promoted as glamorous or fun. Peer group pressure is another powerful influence.

What are the symptoms?
See different ailments.

Who can get them?
Anyone who smokes.

Prevention
The most effective way of giving up smoking is not to start. Be consistent and polite — 'I don't smoke, thanks', is *all* you need to say — there is no need to be drawn into arguments or discussions. Fortunately, more and more people are becoming aware of the dangers of smoking and non-smoking areas in restaurants, etc. are becoming increasingly common.

How to stop
- Drink a large amount of water (about eight glasses per day) between meals. This helps to flush the nicotine out of the body.
- Conserve your mental energy while giving up. Keep regular hours and get plenty of rest.
- Fresh fruit and raw vegetables help to neutralise and eliminate the nicotine in the system.
- Take daily supplements of vitamin C and vitamin B complex.
- Suggested homeopathic remedies:
  Nux vomica and caladium, alternated every four hours, will

help to detoxify the system and reduce the craving for tobacco.

Plantago is also useful, as it makes you feel sick when you smoke.

Kali phos (potassium phosphate) and mag phos (magnesium phosphate) taken four times a day, are also recommended when giving up smoking.

- Tea, coffee, alcohol and cola drinks destabilise the nervous system and make it more difficult to stop smoking, so try to replace them with herb teas or fruit juice.
- Deep breathing and exercise are also helpful — try to take a good walk, breathing deeply in the fresh air, after at least one meal a day.
- Three Bach Flower remedies which may be helpful in giving up smoking are: centaury, for those who naturally weak-willed; cerato, for those who lack confidence in their own ability; and gentian, for those who are easily discouraged.
- Positive thinking *does* work. Say to yourself over and over again, 'I am happier not smoking, I am healthier not smoking, I do not want to smoke,' or similar phrases. If you can convince yourself that you simply do not want to smoke, your battle will be almost over.
- Many people have found acupuncture extremely helpful when giving up smoking. It causes the release of endorphins, which are substances in the brain which give a natural 'high'. It also helps to regulate and balance the body.

SNAKE BITES — see FIRST AID SECTION

SNORING

What is it?
The noise produced during sleep, when the tongue hits the palate and the sleeper breathes through the mouth.

What are the causes?
Snoring is caused by the tongue vibrating against the soft palate of the mouth while sleeping flat on one's back.

What are the symptoms?
The distinctive (and, to the reluctant listener, often infuriating) sound of disturbed breathing through the mouth.

Who can get it?
It is commonly believed that more men than women snore, but there is no evidence to support this claim!

Prevention
There are numerous 'folk remedies' to cure or prevent snoring, but the only real preventative measure is to try to avoid sleeping on one's back.

Treatment
- Suggested homeopathic remedies:
  Nitricum acidum: when snoring is associated with breathlessness.
  Nux vomica: the breathing may be shallow and there may be a feeling of fullness in the stomach.
- Osteopathic or chiropractic manipulation and acupuncture sometimes bring good results. Practising the Alexander Technique may also help to encourage proper breathing, day and night.

SORE THROAT

What is it?
A painful condition of the throat.

What are the causes?
- Too much mucus-forming food.
- Lack of vitamin C or other vital nutrients.
- Over-consumption of refined carbohydrates or of acidic foods.
- Being overtired and run down.
- Smoking and lack of fresh air.
- Any of these factors may give rise to an infection which causes further inflammation or soreness.

What are the symptoms?
They start with a tickling irritation in the throat and develop into a painful throat and, often, a cold or 'flu'. If there is also a rash or fever, follow the treatment suggested under 'Fever' on p. 92.

Who can get it?
Sore throats are common, particularly in children.

How can it be prevented?

- Avoid excessive mucus forming foods, such as dairy products.
- Eat a predominantly vegetarian diet.
- Take adequate exercise in the fresh air.
- Sleep in a well ventilated room.
- Take a daily supplement of vitamin C.
- Avoid overeating.
- Do not smoke.
- Make sure you have sufficient rest, relaxation and sleep.

Treatment

- A mixture of warm salt water, a tbsp of oil (sesame, linseed or olive) and a drop of tabasco makes a very good gargling lotion.
- Take 10-20 g vitamin C per day for a few days combined with bioflavonoids.
- Massage the essential oils of lemon, geranium, hyssop, sage or thyme, individually or mixed, onto the outside of the throat, or inhale them by putting a few drops of the oils in a bowl of boiling water and breathing in the vapour.
- Apply firm and strong massage to the acupoints baihui (Gv 20), dazhui (Gv 14), hegu (Co 4) and wenliu (Co 7) (see p. 165).
- Suggested homeopathic remedies:
  Ammonium causticum: for loss of voice and a burning, raw throat.
  Baptisia: for ulceration, with an offensive odour from the mouth and throat.
  Baryta carbonica: when the sore throat develops slowly and the tonsils are infected. Glands are swollen and there is pain on swallowing.
  Belladonna atropa: acute sore throat, fever and pain on swallowing, throat dry and red. Tonsils swollen. Worse on the right side.
  Capsicum: for sore throats in smokers and heavy drinkers.
  Cantharis: for burning from mouth to stomach, with a highly inflamed throat.
  Cistus canadensis: considerable dryness. Patient has to get up in the night to drink. Feels like sand in the throat. Glands swollen.
  Dulcamara: raw, soreness and burning pains; thick, sticky saliva.
  Guaiacum: violent burning in throat. Throat feels hot. Tonsils swollen and inflamed with a tendency to suppurate. Worse on right side, and with heat, cold weather and touch.

Ignatia amara: for a lump in the throat and a sticky sensation relieved by swallowing.
Lachesis: when the left tonsil is blue and swollen. Pain is worse on swallowing.

- If there is also a headache or pus on the tonsils, fever or other serious symptoms, a physician should be called. Recurring sore throats are another sign that there is something more seriously wrong, which requires professional attention.

STROKES

What are they?
A stroke occurs when either a small clot of blood becomes stuck in a blood vessel in the brain, or a small cerebral blood vessel becomes weakened and breaks down. The second type is usually much more serious, but in either case there is a loss of blood supply to a part of the brain.

What are the causes?
- Arteriosclerosis and atherosclerosis.
- High blood pressure.
- Cigarette smoking.
- Lack of vitamin C and certain other nutrients.
- Excess intake of saturated fats or salt.
- Failure to relax and cope with stress.
- Lack of regular exercise.
- Diabetes.
- Obesity.

What are the symptoms?
In a mild case there may be temporary loss of balance, confusion, inability to speak clearly, impairment of vision or loss of power in a hand or foot. These symptoms usually clear up within a week or two. In more serious cases there may be loss of consciousness, vomiting, headache, and long-term impairment of speech and/or memory, plus loss of movement in one limb or one side of the body. Strokes can also be fatal.

Who can get them?
Older people, and more often men than women.

Prevention
- Attend to any of the factors under 'Causes' which are relevant.
- See recommendations for prevention of arterial disease, on p. 39.
- Eat a well-balanced diet with plenty of fresh fruit.
- Avoid getting angry and over-excited — learn to relax.
- Do not take added salt with your food.

Treatment
- If a stroke occurs, lie the patient down (preferably in bed) with the head a little higher than the feet.
- Place the patient in the recovery position (see p. 162) if unconscious and call for professional help.
- Immediately after the stroke give the homeopathic remedy arnica for shock and thereafter give gelsemium twice a day for at least two weeks.
- Give the following daily supplements: vitamin B complex, choline and inositol, vitamin C and bioflavonoids, vitamin E and lecithin.
- Acupuncture with electro-stimulation is usually helpful.
- Encourage the patient to visualise movement in the paralysed areas of the body.
- Hydrotherapy is also recommended. If possible, arrange for the patient to have exercise therapy in a swimming pool.

SUNBURN

What is it?
A painful skin condition caused by over-exposure to the ultraviolet (UV) rays of the sun.

What are the causes?
The UV rays of the sun are normally absorbed into the pigment produced naturally by the skin as a response. However, if the skin cells have not had enough time to produce adequate pigmentation, the skin will be burnt by the UV rays (hence the importance of only staying in the sun for a short time during the first days on holiday). Do not be fooled into thinking that the weather has to be bright and sunny for the skin to be affected — the sun's rays can be just as dangerous on an overcast day. UV rays combined with salt water from swimming in the sea and/or a strong wind can be particularly dangerous.

What are the symptoms?

The affected skin will feel hot and look red. The sufferer will feel 'itchy' and possibly faint or giddy. Severe sunburn can cause blistering, dehydration and, possibly, sunstroke.

Who can get it?

Those with fairer skins have less natural pigment and so are more prone to burning. They should take especial care.

Prevention

- Expose yourself to the sun gradually. If you have a fair skin start with no more than twenty minutes in a strong sun.
- It is better to avoid the midday sun at first and stick to early morning and late afternoon for sunbathing. Fair or freckled skins should *always* avoid the midday sun.
- Use a suncream with a sunblock. The numbering systems may vary according to the brand name, but the only rule to remember is that the fairer your skin, the higher the sunblock number should be.
- Take a supplement of vitamin C (1 g a day) and PABA (1 g a day) for a few days prior to your first exposure to strong sunlight. (PABA is a component of folic acid, and is available in healthfood shops.)

Treatment

- Soak the area with cold water or apply cold water compresses.
- For severe sunburn, see treatment for 'Burns' on p. 153.
- Take additional vitamins A (25,000 IU a day), PABA (1 g a day), C (3 g a day), D (3,000 IU a day), E (500 IU a day) and calcium (1 g a day).
- Apply the juice of aloe vera or fresh lemon.
- Suggested homeopathic remedies:
  Kalium carbonicum: generally useful for sunburn.
  Bufo: if the face tans too quickly.
  Cantharis: useful in severe cases of sunburn. Take the remedy four times a day for a day or two.

TETANUS

What is it?

A dangerous condition in which there is spasmodic contraction of all the muscles in the body, starting in the jaws (hence its other name, lockjaw). It is associated with a bacterium which is frequently found in cultivated soil and which gains entry to the body via a wound.

What are the causes?
A wound which becomes infected because of poor hygiene — often through dirty soil.

What are the symptoms?
The first symptoms are painful spasms of the muscles of the jaw and back of neck, which occur about eight days after a wound has become infected. The mouth cannot be opened, and the other muscles in the body subsequently become affected.

Who can get it?
Anyone. Those who work out of doors are perhaps more at risk.

Prevention
- Thorough cleansing of all wounds.
- Give the homeopathic remedy hypericum after any deep cut.

Treatment
- Immediately, give several doses of the Bach Flowers Rescue Remedy.
- Give the homeopathic remedies ledum palustre and hypericum every twenty minutes in the early stages.
- Give large amounts of vitamin C for the first few days.
- If anti-tetanus serum has been advised, give the homeopathic remedy sulphur just before the injection and thuja occidentalis afterwards.

THRUSH

What is it?
An inflammation or infection of certain areas where there is mucous membrane, e.g. in the vagina (vaginitis), in the mouth or on the nails. Vaginitis is the most common.

What are the causes?
Thrush is caused by over-production of the fungus *candida* in various parts of the body. Many factors affect the candida fungus, including:

- Antibiotics.
- Vitamin B deficiency, especially B6.
- Intestinal worms.
- Tight-fitting synthetic underwear.
- Diabetes.
- Excess sugar in the bloodstream.
- Poor hygiene.
- Cystitis.
- Sexual intercourse with someone who has the fungus.
- Frequent douching of the vagina.
- Stress.
- Allergies.

What are the symptoms?
- In vaginal thrush, there is a profuse, offensive and curdy discharge with irritation and itching. Sexual intercourse is painful.
- In the mouth, thrush appears as creamy white patches on an inflamed lining inside the cheeks, on the lips and on the gums.
- On the nails, thrush appears as damaged cuticles and unsightly nails.
- Babies sometimes have a thrush rash around the back passage.

Who can get it?
Those who are generally run down are more prone to thrush. For vaginal thrush, women whose personal hygiene is of a low standard and/or those with many sexual partners — it is very contagious — are more at risk.

Prevention (vaginal thrush)
- See prevention of Cystitis (p. 79).
- Wear cotton underwear.
- Do not take the contraceptive pill — it depletes vitamins from the body.
- Eat natural, live yoghurt every day.
- Pay particular attention to personal hygiene. Women should always wipe themselves from front to back with toilet tissue, to avoid spreading infection.

Treatment (vaginal thrush)
- Check that you haven't left a tampon in place.
- Take the following supplements every day:
  Vitamin A (50,000 IU a day).
  Vitamin B6 (50 mg, twice a day).

Vitamin B complex (100 mg, twice a day).
Vitamin C (1-5 g a day).
Vitamin E (300 mg, twice a day).
Zinc orotate (200 mg, twice a day).
(The vitamin B supplement must be non-yeast based if there is a candida infection).

- Take garlic every day — in capsule or perle form if you dislike the smell.
- Eat natural live yoghurt daily and also apply a little to the vagina morning and evening. This is best introduced with a tampon inserter.
- Take Super Dophilus tablets daily.
- Douch with one tbsp of tea tree oil to a litre of warm water, twice a day. Alternatively, douch with apple cider vinegar (two tbsps in a pint of warm water).
- Do not drink tea, coffee or alcohol and avoid chocolate, sugar, mushrooms and bread.
- Use a good lubricant when you have sexual intercourse.
- Suggested homeopathic remedies:
  Aconitum napellus: when the vagina is hot, dry and sensitive, or menstrual bleeding often lasts a long time, or is too late.
  Belladonna atropa: vagina hot and dry. Bright, red, profuse, offensive menstrual periods which often arrive early.
  Pulsatilla nigricans: useful for vaginitis during pregnancy.
  Graphites: for a thin, white, burning discharge, which may be increased by walking, or in the morning.

The dietary recommendations given here will also help other forms of thrush.

TINNITUS — see EARACHE AND EAR PROBLEMS

TONSILLITIS — see SORE THROAT

TOOTHACHE

What is it?
Pain in and around the teeth.

What are the causes?

There are three main causes of toothache: tooth decay, gum disease and abcesses.

When particles of food, particularly sugary or starchy (carbohydrate) foods, are left in the mouth for more than twelve hours, they start to form plaque — the sticky substance which adheres to the teeth and causes tooth decay.

The bacteria in plaque produce an acid which erodes the teeth and causes the gums to bleed. Gum disease can lead to the loss of teeth, when the gums eventually start to recede and the teeth loosen.

Toothache can also be caused by abscesses, which require urgent treatment by a dentist.

What are the symptoms?

The pain will vary in length and intensity according to the cause, but there will be pain. The jaw may ache, particularly if there is an abscess present.

Who can get it?

Most cases of toothache are entirely unnecessary and could have been prevented by proper dental hygiene.

Prevention

- Do not eat sweets, sugary food or refined carbohydrates. 'Fizzy' drinks are particularly harmful to teeth because of the noxious combination of acid and sugar they contain.
- Ensure that you have a balanced and healthy diet with adequate vitamin and mineral intake.
- Alfalfa tablets taken daily will help to prevent dental decay.
- Brush the teeth regularly before and after meals. Make sure that the bristles enter the small groove of gum tissue that surrounds each tooth. Using dental floss and toothpicks will also help keep the teeth free from particles of food.

Treatment

- Continue to carry out the steps listed under 'Prevention' above. Acute toothache may be treated by applying oil of cloves to the tooth, or chewing a clove slowly over the aching tooth.
- Massaging the gums with eucalyptus oil or witch hazel once a day helps with gum disease, as does massaging the gums with vitamin E oil.
- Suggested homeopathic remedies:
  Aconitum napellus: when the pain is worse in cold wind, but better with cold water.

Arnica montana: for filled teeth.

Chamomilla: when the pain is worse in cold air and with hot drinks.

Magnesia phosphorica: this often helps with throbbing toothache.

Mercuris sulphuricus: for a stabbing pain radiating out to the ears. Worse at night.

Silicea: for pain which is worse with hot or cold food or cold wind and is often worse at night. It may be associated with an abscess.

Staphysagria: for severe pain with teeth sensitive to the slightest touch.

TRAVEL SICKNESS

What is it?
Nausea and vomiting when travelling in a vehicle. It may occur in trains, planes, cars, boats, ships or on fairground or playground apparatus, such as roundabouts or swings.

What are the causes?
The differing input of information from the eyes and the balance mechanism in the ears causes confusion and dizziness. There may also be emotional factors.

What are the symptoms?
Feelings of giddiness, nausea and possibly actual vomiting. There may also be dizziness, headaches or fainting episodes.

Who can get it?
Travel sickness occurs mainly in children, who usually grow out of it.

Prevention
Prevention and treatment are more or less the same. Reassurance and distraction are helpful in the case of children.

Treatment
- Avoid over-excitement or anxiety before travelling.
- Take vitamin B6 (20 mg) on the day prior to travel and hourly during the journey.
- Suck a piece of ginger root, if you do not find it too strong, or a slice of lemon.

- Press regularly on the acupoint neiguan (P6) (see p. 170) throughout the journey.
- Suggested homeopathic remedies:
  Petroleum: if usually fine when driving, but sick when a passenger; better for eating; worse in damp weather and in winter; better in warm air.
  Cocculus indicus: if better when lying down; worse after eating; worse with window open or when cold; there is nausea when looking at a boat in motion. There may be aversion to food and loss of appetite.
  Staphysagria: very sensitive. A child will cry for many things and refuse them when given. Hungry, craves stimulants. Better for warmth.
  Borax: if very susceptible to downward motion, e.g. in a lift, or when there are 'air pockets'. Worse in warm weather and in the morning.
  Rhus toxicodendrum: for nausea, dizziness and bloated abdomen. Worse in cold, wet weather and when resting. Better walking or moving or changing position.

ULCERS

What are they?
Ulcers are inflamed patches — characteristically appearing as small depressions — on the skin surface or internally. (See also Mouth Ulcers, p. 119 and Bedsores, p. 53).

What are the causes?
They are caused by a defect in normal bodily functions — in the case of ulcers on the legs, they are frequently the result of varicose veins, where blood is not circulating properly around the legs. Internal (peptic) ulcers are caused by over-production of acid and enzymes in the stomach.

What are the symptoms?
Skin ulcers can be recognized with the appearance of red, painful patches which do not heal. Internal ulcers cause severe burning pain in one particular area, most noticeable after cooking certain foods (often spicy or acidic). There may be sickness.

Who can get them?
Internal ulcers occur more in men than women, particularly older men. Skin ulcers are common in those who are immobile —

e.g. the elderly — who may well also be constipated, thus heightening the risk of poor circulation.

Prevention
- Do not smoke.
- Do not eat large quantities of acidic foods or very highly spiced foods.
- Try to deal with stress before it becomes a real problem — it is certainly a contributory factor to peptic ulcers.

Treatment (Internal ulcers)
- Stop smoking, if you still do.
- Do not drink coffee or tea, or alcohol. Comfrey tea is a good substitute.
- Do not eat refined foods, and avoid highly seasoned or fried food.
- Deal with constipation if it is present.
- Drink four to five glasses a day of fresh vegetable juice, made with half cabbage juice and half celery, beetroot or carrot juice.
- Drink slippery elm bark three times a day. This can be obtained as a powder from healthfood shops and made into a hot drink.
- Take daily supplements of vitamins A, C and E and of zinc.
- Do not allow stress to build up — take up meditation or buy a relaxation tape if you need to unwind.
- Massage the acupoints baihui (Gv 20), zhongwang (Ren 12), neiguan (P 6) and zusanli (St 36) (see p. 165).
- Suggested homeopathic remedies:
  Anacardium orientale: always better immediately after eating, but usually has pain two hours afterwards.
  Argentum nitricum: for flatulence and gnawing pains in the pit of the stomach, which become worse with food and pressure. There is a craving for sugar and sweet foods which usually aggravates the disorder. A strongly nervous, phobic element is associated with this remedy.
  Atropinum: for severe mid-abdominal pains with associated nausea and vomiting. Usually better with food.
  Kalium bichromicum: for nausea, vomiting and mucus with burning pains, which are usually worse after eating.
  Sulphur: for hunger pains around 11 am.
  Condurango: for pain behind the breast bone with the feeling that food is stuck there.

Treatment (Skin ulcers)
- See the treatment for Boils on p. 57.

- Apply a dressing with a mixture of honey and crushed garlic on the *outside*. Cover with a little cotton wool and bandage lightly in position over the ulcer.
- Apply vitamin E cream or oil (best done by breaking open a capsule) to the ulcer. If the ulcer is resistant to treatment it may be necessary to obtain professional help.

VAGINITIS — see THRUSH

VARICOSE VEINS

What are they?
Lumpy, protruding veins in the legs. They occur when the valves in the legs stop fulfilling their normal function, which is to help send the circulating blood back up the legs, towards the heart. When the 'stopped' blood collects, it distends the veins.

What are the causes?
- Constipation.
- Obesity.
- Poor circulation.
- Over consumption of refined foods.
- Bad posture.
- Excessive standing or sitting (often occupational).
- Lack of exercise.
- Pregnancy.
- Liver damage.

What are the symptoms?
Appearance of distended veins, with possible itchiness and swelling of ankles.

Who can get them?
Those predisposed to varicose veins include: pregnant women; those who are overweight and/or constipated; those who have to stand for long periods, e.g. as part of their job.

Prevention
- Avoid being constipated.
- Keep to your correct weight.
- Ensure your posture is correct, both when standing and sitting.

- Take a reasonable amount of exercise every day.

Treatment
- Improve your circulation by taking regular exericse. Frequent short spells of exercise are best for varicose veins, until the condition improves.
- Do not sit cross-legged.
- Deal with constipation.
- Contrast bathing of the legs in hot and cold water is helpful.
- Massage the legs from the ankles upwards with a few drops of rosemary or lavender oil mixed into some almond oil.
- Every day, spend some time with your legs raised higher than the rest of the body. Standing on your head, or any other inverted posture, is excellent if you can manage it.
- Take 200 mg vitamin E three times a day, and take vitamins C and P (500 mg twice a day of each), lecithin (10 mg a day) and rutin (250 mg, twice a day).
- Eat plenty of dandelion leaves, parsley, spinach, mustard greens, and other green vegetables.
- Take two tbsps of wheatgerm and three tsps of brewer's yeast daily.
- Rosemary tea is helpful, as it strengthens the cardiovascular system. Make the tea by adding one tsp of the dried leaves to one cup of boiling water. Steep for five minutes and allow to cool. Drink three cups a day. A little honey may be used to sweeten the tea if desired.
- Do not eat any refined foods or sugar.
- Take garlic in some form every day.
- A small amount of saffron daily helps to rebuild tissue and strengthen the heart.
- Suggested homeopathic remedies:
  Aconitum napellus: when the veins are due to fatigue and long periods of standing.
  Carbo vegetabilis: when they are associated with poor circulation.
  Hammamelis virginica: apply a few drops of mother tincture to the painful vein.
  Pulsatilla nigricans: useful for problems during pregnancy or following childbirth.
  Silicea: for complicated cases, often with infections in some part of the body.

WARTS AND VERRUCAS

What are they?
Small, usually raised, patches of skin which can appear on various parts of the body.

What are the causes?
An infectious virus. They are spread by direct contact. Verrucas (warts on the soles of the feet) are often spread via the floors of swimming-pool changing rooms. However, warts are not highly infectious and by no means everyone catches them. It usually takes some time for them to appear after the virus enters the system.

What are the symptoms?
The appearance of small, often raised, patches of skin. They are usually round in shape and may be of a darker colour than the rest of the skin, i.e. dark red or brown. They occur most frequently on the hands, the knees, the soles of the feet (verrucas) and the genital area.

Who can get them?
Warts on the hand are common amongst schoolchildren. Genital warts, which are contagious, are spread by direct sexual contact and so those with more than one sexual partner may be at greater risk.

Prevention
- Wear rubber shoes at swimming-pools and similar areas.
- Try to avoid hand contact with anyone who obviously has warts on the hands.

Treatment
Warts will drop off eventually, but this may take several years. In the interim, however, proprietary treatments for warts are available and may be effective.
- For relief from pain and irritation, try painting the warts with lemon juice, freshly crushed garlic, or the juice from dandelion or calendula stalks.
- Saliva, applied regularly, can sometimes help to remove warts. But remember that they will eventually disappear of their own accord.

WHOOPING COUGH

What is it?
An infectious disease of the respiratory tract, usually affecting young children.

What are the causes?
A bacterial infection, often occurring in epidemics, which is easily spread via schools, playgroups etc.

What are the symptoms?
Feverish, cold-like symptoms at first, followed at least a week later by the onset of the distinctive 'whooping' sound — caused when the child coughs uncontrollably and then gasps for air afterwards. There is often some sickness afterwards. The coughing fits may last for some weeks.

Who can get it?
Children. The disease is more serious in young children and babies, as they find it even more difficult to breathe than older children. Babies may have to be admitted to hospital.

Prevention
- Early vaccination is often advised as the illness is more serious for babies, but there has been much controversy over the possible side effects, particularly if the child or anyone in the family has suffered any form of neurological damage or convulsions. Parents are therefore advised to think carefully before deciding.
- If there is an epidemic, give the homeopathic remedy drosera, night and morning for a week, or pertussin, once a day.

Treatment
- In very young children, always consult a practitioner.
- Give the homeopathic remedy drosera, for coughing and vomiting.
- Give the child a vitamin C supplement daily.
- Ensure the child drinks plenty of fluid, and avoid dry foods which may aggravate coughing.
- Rub the chest with eucalyptus oil or Olbas Oil, readily available from herbalists, to ease breathing.

WIND — see FLATULENCE

FIRST AID

The following section covers those situations when immediate help is needed after an unexpected accident. By combining traditional First Aid practices with holistic remedies to promote the body's natural healing processes, you will give the body the best possible chance to recover.

ANIMAL BITES

Animal bites are fairly rare but should always be treated with caution and seen by a doctor, as there may be a risk of tetanus (see p. 136)

Treatment (homeopathic)
- Always cleanse the bite with hypericum. Pure tincture may be used, or it can be diluted with cold, boiled water.
- Take ledum 30, twice a day, for two or three days.
- If there is swelling and pain, take apis 6x.

BANDAGING

Knowing how to apply bandages correctly is an essential part of First Aid treatment. They can prevent blood loss, hold a fractured limb in place, reduce swelling, provide support for broken limbs and prevent infection, so are extremely useful 'remedies'. Every home First Aid box (see p. 191) should contain several bandages.

Bandages can be made from flannel, cotton (calico), elastic net or special types of paper, or they may be improvised in emergencies from stockings, scarves, handkerchiefs, ties etc. If the bandage is to come in contact with a wound, it is preferable to boil the material first, if time allows. Where bleeding is profuse it is more important to stem the flow of blood, and applying pressure with an improvised dressing is better than no dressing at all.

Obviously, bandages differ according to the functions they are required to perform and the nature of the injury they are being used for. The simplest bandage is a thin strip of loose woven cotton, used to tie a dressing into place over a cut or wound. Dressings are sterile layers of gauze, often incorporating cotton wool. Sometimes, the dressing is covered with cotton wool before being bandaged into place in order to provide additional protection to the wound.

HOW TO APPLY A BANDAGE

Have the casualty sitting or lying down. Ensure any injured part is well supported and is in the position in which it should remain.

Bandages should be firm enough to keep a dressing in place, but not so tight that they interfere with circulation. If in doubt, check a pulse that lies further away from the body than the bandage. Also check the fingers or toes for coldness, blueness and lack of voluntary movement. A further test for circulation is to press on a fingernail or toenail, which will cause a white appearance underneath the nail. When you release the pressure, the normal redness or pink colour should return immediately. If this does not happen, the bandage is too tight.

BANDAGING A HAND OR FOOT

- Support the hand in a palm down position by having someone holding the wrist, if possible. When bandaging a foot, the lower part of the leg should be supported on a stool or suitable object so that the foot is free.
- Place the end of a tubular bandage on the wrist or above the ankle and make one turn of the bandage around the wrist or leg to anchor it.

BANDAGING A HAND

- Bring the bandage diagonally over the back of the hand excluding the thumb, to the level of the base of the little finger, then continue taking it underneath the fingers to wrap round at the level of the base of the nail of the little finger.
  In the case of the foot, follow the same principle, but treat the big toe in the same manner as the other toes and do not exclude it in the way that the thumb is excluded (see diagram on previous page).
- Keeping the bandage tight, now change direction and bring the bandage diagonally over the back of the hand or foot towards the wrist or ankle (see diagram).
- Continue with these figure-of-eight turns until the entire hand or foot is covered.
- Finish with another turn round the wrist or ankle, secure the end and check for circulation, as above.

BANDAGING AN ELBOW OR KNEE

- Have the limb supported in the most comfortable position. Place the end of the bandage on the outside of the knee or elbow, and make a single turn.
- Next, make a turn around the limb just above the elbow or knee so that it covers half the first turn. Follow this with another turn below the joint, covering the other half of the first turn.
- Repeat this process, allowing each turn of the bandage to cover slightly more than two thirds of the previous one.
- Finish with two turns directly over the elbow or knee, secure the end and check for circulation.

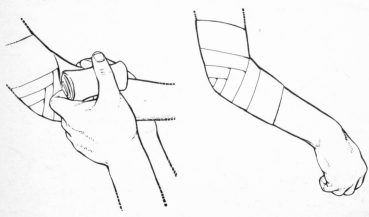

BANDAGING AN ELBOW

BANDAGING THE HEAD

1 Fold a hem along the base of a triangular bandage, or scarf in an emergency. Place this on the casualty's forehead just above the eyebrows.

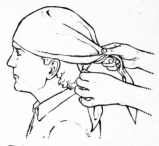

2 Bring the ends round to the back of the head, keeping them above the ears.

3 Cross the ends over the apex of the bandage at the nape of the neck and bring them round to the front of the head. Tie the ends with a reef knot (see note) on the forehead just below the hair line.

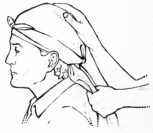

4 Support the head with your left hand (or your right, if left-handed) and gently pull the apex or point of the bandage to take up any excess material.

5 Bring the apex to the top of the head and secure it, with a safety pin, to the underlying bandage.

Note: A reef knot is tied by taking the two ends and crossing the left hand strand over the right hand one and tucking it underneath. The two ends are taken again and the right hand one is now crossed over the left hand one and also tucked underneath. When the two ends are pulled, a reef knot is formed.

APPLYING A SLING

MAKING A SLING

A sling is the best way to protect and support the upper arm or the chest.

To make a simple arm sling, make sure the patient is sitting or standing and the injured arm supported. The wrist and hand should be slightly higher than the elbow (see illustration).

Slide one end of a triangular bandage between the chest and forearm so that the point of the bandage reaches well below the elbow. Place the upper end of the bandage over the non-damaged shoulder, around the neck and back down to the front of the injured side.

Continue to support the forearm. Bring the lower end of the bandage over the hand and forearm. Tie a reef knot near the shoulder (see note p. 151). Secure the remaining part of the bandage with a safety pin.

BROKEN BONES

There are two types of broken bone (fracture) — closed fractures, where the surrounding skin is not broken, and open fractures, where the broken bone has punctured the skin's surface and protrudes outside it. In both cases, the immediate aim is to keep the fractured area immobile, call for urgent medical help and comfort the patient.

Treatment

- Do not move the patient if a fracture is suspected. Call for immediate professional help and keep the patient immobile.
- If the patient is in shock, give a few drops of the Bach Flowers Rescue Remedy (see p. 17).
- For all fractures, a small magnet applied to the area of the fracture will accelerate union and healing. Hold it in place with a loose bandage.
- For painful fractures, give asafoetida 6 or 6x.
- Give a supplement of comfrey, alfalfa, calcium, phosphorus, magnesium, potassium and vitamin C.
- If the fracture is not healing give calcarea phosphorica and calcarea fluorica. Symphytum taken once per day for two or three weeks is also recommended.

BRUISES

A bruise occurs when the skin remains intact but a blood vessel becomes damaged as a result of a blow, knock or other injury. The internal bleeding produces discolouration, swelling and tenderness.

Treatment

- If it is only a minor bruise apply arnica ointment. In more serious cases, apply a tight bandage soaked in arnica solution (ten drops of tincture to a cupful of cold water). Ice may also be applied over the bruise.
- Massage gently from the edge of the bruise towards the centre of the body.
- Take arnica montana. This is an excellent remedy for all kinds of bruising.

BURNS AND SCALDS

A burn is an injury to the body tissue, caused by heat, chemicals or radiation. The latter includes burns caused by electricity. Intense cold may also cause a burn though this is rare in most parts of the world. Severe burns may cause shock and infection to set in.

Burns are usually classified into three types:

First degree burns: confined to superficial layers of skin. There is redness, tenderness and sometimes swelling.

Second degree burns: several layers of skin are involved. Blisters, inflammation and swelling occur. The danger of infection exists and the wound must be covered with a sterile dressing.

Third degree burns: All the layers of skin and possibly some underlying structures are involved. May be less painful than more superficial burns because of nerve damage. The patient must receive medical attention.

If more than 9 per cent of the body is involved in any burn, it is necessary to call for medical attention immediately.

Treatment

Immediate action: if the hair or clothing is on fire, smother in a blanket or large cloth. Call an ambulance straightaway.

- If the burn is not severe, immerse the area in cold water (not ice), for ten minutes, or longer if the pain persists.
- Apply hypericum lotion (about ten drops of mother tincture to a cup of water) to the burn.
- Give one dose of arnica montana or a few drops of the Bach Flowers Rescue Remedy (p. 17). Urtica urens is useful in minor cases where there is blistering.
- In all serious burns, 1 g of vitamin C an hour should be given for the first day. Other important nutrients for burns are vitamins A, B complex, E and F, plus zinc and calcium.
- Never apply any sort of ointment or cream to skin which has just been burned. Once the skin has started to heal up, however, vitamin E cream (or oil, direct from capsules) can be applied to the burns.

CHOKING

Treatment

Choking happens when the body's air passages become blocked by food or a foreign object, or when something gets into the windpipe rather than going down the normal passage to the stomach. It is vital that the item is dislodged as quickly as possible to avoid asphyxiation. The casualty may be panicking.

- Grasp the casualty around the waist from behind, with your left hand made into a fist and your thumb pressing under their rib cage. Place your right hand over the left and press sharply into the casualty's abdomen with an inward and upward thrust. Repeat two or three times.
- Give the Bach Flowers Rescue Remedy.

CUTS AND GRAZES

MINOR CUTS

Minor cuts happen regularly and are usually of no consequence. However, it is important to ensure that they do not become infected, as tetanus (see p. 136) can set in.

Cleanse the cut in running water and wash the edges with warm soapy water if dirty. Apply calendula ointment or soak with tincture of calendula. Cover if indicated. Keep applying the ointment or tincture until the cut is healing up well.

MAJOR CUTS

These are usually caused by metal or glass and cut not only the skin, but the structures under the skin. This can cause permanent damage, so it is important to take special care when using dangerous tools or machinery.

Treatment

- Remove any foreign matter from the cut that can be easily dislodged, without further irritating the wound.
- Thoroughly irrigate the cut with cold or warm *boiled* water to which a few drops of hypericum have been added (about ten drops of the mother tincture to a cupful of water).
- If the cut is bleeding badly, continued firm pressure on the site of the bleeding should help stop the flow of blood.
- Try to avoid having stitches if possible. Very often they are not needed, and dumbbell dressings which pull the sides of the wound together may work just as well.
- Apply a dressing soaked in the hypericum solution as above. Replace this every half hour until the cut seems to be healing. Do not allow the dressing to dry out.
- Suggested homeopathic remedies:
  Take arnica every ten minutes for the first hour, every twenty minutes for the next hour, every half hour for two hours and hourly thereafter for one or two days.
  If there is laceration (torn flesh) hypericum should also be taken.
  Ledum should be taken if there is any likelihood of catching tetanus. In this case, it should be taken two or three times a day for a few days.
- If stitches have been put in, take rhus toxicodendrum twice a day for three days, or if in low potency, every four hours for three days.

DROWNING

Clearly the aim here is to prevent death by asphyxiation from water in the lungs. As such, emergency First Aid treatment should be given immediately.

Treatment

- Remove any obstruction to the airways. Begin mouth-to-mouth resuscitation (see p. 158) immediately — in the water if possible. Continue for as long as necessary.
- Give the Bach Flower Rescue Remedy and aconitum napellus (two or three doses).
- As soon as the casualty starts to breathe again, place in the recovery position (see p. 162) and remove wet clothing. Keep them warm and dry until medical help arrives.

ELECTRIC SHOCK

The effects of the passage of an electric current, usually from the main electricity supply in a home, through the body, will cause what is known as electric shock. It can also be caused by lightning, railway cables, etc.

The electricity current in most homes causes the muscles to contract many times per second and can be very damaging, often causing severe subsequent burns, especially if your hands are wet and if you are standing on the ground or on a metal step. Higher voltages, e.g. railway currents, may be more damaging or even fatal. Great care should always be taken when working with electrical apparatus and/or if there are young children in the house.

Treatment

- Always switch off the current if the casualty is still connected. NEVER touch the person directly. If the current cannot be broken, and a muscle spasm is preventing the patient from letting go, push or pull the person away from the source using a non-conducting material such as paper or wood (e.g. a walking stick, wooden rolling pin or rolled-up newspaper).
- An alternative is to loop a piece of rope or pair of tights around the casualty's ankles and pull it. Stand on a rubber mat, or wear wellingtons if possible, while doing so.

N.B. — If the casualty has been affected by very high voltage currents, e.g. from railway lines, do not attempt to move until the power is cut off by the appropriate authorities. Call emergency help and keep well away from the casualty.

- Next, check for heartbeat and breathing. Apply mouth to mouth resuscitation (see p. 158) if necessary. Otherwise, place the casualty in the recovery position (see p. 160)
- Treat the casualty for shock and give a little Bach Flowers Rescue Remedy (p. 17).
- If there are burns, these should now be treated (see p. 153).
- Get medical help. This is essential if the casualty is unconscious.

EMERGENCIES

An emergency can be defined as a situation where one or more people have suffered serious, or potentially serious, injuries and may be at further risk if not given immediate First Aid. Fires, bomb blasts and road accidents are examples of emergencies.

Treatment
- Immediate treatment — give arnica montana 30 immediately, followed shortly afterwards by hypericum 30. One small pill is enough. A tincture is better for unconscious patients, or a few drops of Bach Flower Rescue Remedy smeared around the lips.
- The traditional First Aid steps should then be carried out. Check first for respiration and heart beat. If respiration has stopped, give mouth-to-mouth resuscitation (see illustrations overleaf):

1 Place the casualty flat, face up.
2 Tilt the head back to straighten the airways.
3 Remove any obvious obstruction, e.g. swallowed objects or false teeth, but without wasting unnecessary time.
4 Pinch the nose, take a deep breath and cover the casualty's mouth with your lips, taking care to seal them completely around the mouth.
5 Breathe firmly into the casualty's mouth.
6 Remove your mouth and take another breath.
7 Repeat the process. The rate of inflations should be about 15 a minute.

STAGES OF MOUTH-TO-MOUTH RESUSCITATION

1 Clearing the airway. Tilt the patient's head to one side and remove any obvious obstructions, such as dentures, loose teeth, food or vomit. Also loosen any constrictions around the neck, such as ties or collars.

2 Hold the head well back, supporting it under the neck with one hand. Open the mouth as wide as possible, and use your other hand to pinch the nostrils shut.

3 (*Left*) Take a deep breath, cover the patient's mouth with yours, and blow firmly into it, at the same time keeping the nose closed by pinching the nostrils. Remove your mouth, take another breath, then repeat the inflation.

- In the case of a child, cover the nose and mouth with your lips. Breathe more gently and inflate at the rate of 20 times a minute. For an infant, seal the nose and mouth but only inflate using air from your mouth — do NOT use air from your lungs.
- CARDIAC MASSAGE. If the casualty shows no sign of breathing after four inflations, check the pulse. If there is none, undertake instant cardiac massage: place both hands (locked one over the other) over the centre of the breastbone and press rhythmically about eighty times a minute. Rock your body to and fro as you do so, but do not move your hands (see illustration opposite). For small children, one hand is sufficient and a faster rate of 90-100 times a minute should be maintained.
- Now, check for bleeding. If external, apply pressure with a dressing or pad of cloth direct to the wound. See p. 155 for further details. Internal bleeding may be suggested by an

CARDIAC MASSAGE

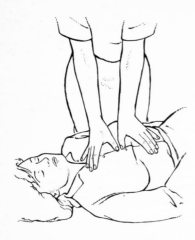 

1 Finding the massage point. Lay the casualty face up on a firm surface. Kneel or stand alongside. The right point to apply pressure is roughly halfway between the sternal notch at the top of the breastbone, and the intersection of the ribs at the bottom.

2 Locking your hands together over the massage point, lean forward until your arms are vertical. Press down firmly but gently, then rock back to release the pressure. Repeat this movement at the rate of approximately 80 per minute, rocking your body in rhythm.

increased pulse rate, weak pulse, pale face and lips or cold and clammy skin. The casualty may be restless and thirsty and possibly nauseous. There may be gasping and yawning. Urgent medical treatment is needed for internal bleeding, but in the meantime, continue with the hypericum and also give phosphorus 30.

- Suggested homeopathic remedies:
If there is injury to a bone, give symphytum 6×. For bone pain, give conium 30. If there is injury to the spine, give ruta graveolens 6x. When the membrane covering a bone is damaged, give ruta graveolens. If there is trembling after an accident, give sticta 30. In all cases, continue to give hyper-icum at frequent intervals. Even long after an accident, arnica 30 will be effective, as will the Bach Flower remedies Rock Rose and Star of Bethlehem.
- When the casualty is conscious, place in recovery position (see pp. 161-162). Keep casualty warm.

HEAD INJURIES

Head injuries are potentially very serious as they carry the risk of brain damage. Take careful note of all symptoms for the doctor or hospital. They usually result from a fall, or a blow to the head. There may be concussion, or pain in the head. Bleeding from the ears, eyes or mouth normally indicates a fracture.

Treatment
- Check breathing and heartbeat — if no signs, follow the emergency procedures on pp. 157-159.
- Never leave the casualty on their back. Always place in the recovery position, or at least on their side. Prop the jaw open to prevent the casualty from inhaling vomit or blood.
- If there has been any period of unconsciousness, or if there is an obvious fracture, call for immediate medical help.
- Give arnica montana and hypericum immediately. Subsequently, give arnica every four hours and hypericum if there is any bleeding.
- Check for signs of internal bleeding, such as increasing lethargy, a change in the pulse rate, forceful vomiting, unequal pupils, or a deep sleep, which may be followed by coma.
- If you notice any of these signs, the patient's skull should be X-rayed.
- If the patient has dilated pupils, stiffness of the neck muscles, spasms, twitching of the muscles or mental confusion, give cicuta virosa twice a day, until the symptoms clear up.
- Treat any wounds.
- If there is a persistent headache give natrum sulphuricum 30. A few doses of this remedy should be given to anyone who has had concussion, even some time afterwards.

HEART ATTACKS

May be recognized by intense gripping pain in the chest, possibly radiating to the jaw, throat, arms or back. The face is ashen and the lips may be blue. The casualty will have a rapid, weak pulse and be breathless.

160

Treatment
- If patient is conscious, prop up in a chair or in bed. Do not move.
- Loosen any constricting clothing.
- Give the Bach Flower Rescue Remedy and aconitum napellus.
- In older patients with swollen ankles, give lachesis.
- Apply strong stimulation to the acupoints neiguan (P6), shaochong (H9), shanzhong (Ren 17) and shenmen (H7) (see p. 165).

  With heart failure, resuscitate immediately with external cardiac massage (p. 158).
- After breathing has been restored, place the patient in the recovery position (see below). Summon medical help.

INSECT STINGS

Insect stings are usually very painful, but rarely dangerous. However, some people are allergic to insect stings (most people know when they are), so watch for large swellings or signs of shock (see p. 162), and call for medical attention.

Treatment
- If the sting is still stuck into the skin, remove it with tweezers.
- Apply vinegar, lemon juice, or if necessary, wine, to a wasp sting and bicarbonate of soda to a bee sting.
- Give homeopathic apis if there is swelling and pain. If the bite is very angry-looking take cantharis.
- Give ledum twice per day for two or three days.
- Apply tincture of hypercal to soothe the bite.

THE RECOVERY POSITION

The recovery position should be used when a casualty is breathing and the heart is beating properly. It ensures that the airway is open and that the body is in a comfortable position.

Lay the casualty in the position shown overleaf, with one leg bent to support the body. One arm should be straight down by the side and the other bent up as shown in the illustration.

PATIENT IN RECOVERY POSITION

SHOCK

There are many kinds of shock, but the common feature is that the circulatory system fails to deliver sufficient blood to the body's vital organs, particularly the brain. This is usually caused by the heart pumping inefficiently, following electrocution, blockage of the coronary artery, or other situations. The commonest cause of shock is the small blood vessels suddenly dilating and draining away blood from the heart and brain. This is termed nervous shock and is not a serious condition in that it is not life-threatening. This is the sort of shock that occurs after bad news or narrowly escaping a disaster. Some people may suffer this type of shock when they see blood.

Another common reason for circulatory failure is loss of fluid from bleeding, burns, vomiting or diarrhoea. This is sometimes termed surgical shock and this type of shock is *always* serious. Many deaths from injuries are caused not by the injury itself, but by shock. Prompt First Aid treatment can help reduce shock and may save a life.

How to recognize shock
- The skin is cold and clammy and looks pale. This is most obvious inside the lips.
- The casualty may feel week, faint or giddy.
- The pulse is weak and fast.
- Breathing is shallow and fast.
- The casualty may be anxious and restless and may yawn or gasp due to a need for air.
- There may be thirst, sickness or vomiting.
- The casualty may become unconscious.

Treatment (Nervous shock)
- Keep the casualty calm and warm. Give a few drops of the Bach Flowers Rescue Remedy (p. 17) immediately.
- Suggested homeopathic remedies:
Aconitum napellus: if fear is very marked. This is the remedy for someone escaping from a disaster, such as a fire or accident.
Carbo vegetabilis: when there is a great need for air, a desire to be fanned, coldness and mental torpor.
Opium: for loss of consciousness or the apoplectic state.
Hypericum perforatum: for shock from nervous damage.
Lachesis: when breathing almost stops.
Ignatia amara: for shock following bad news.

Treatment (Surgical shock)
- Stop any bleeding: this is the first priority. Send for professional help. Lay the patient down, loosen their clothing, and remove false teeth or any visible food which may be blocking the mouth or throat. Raise the legs by placing a rolled up coat or similar object under the feet. Ensure that the head is turned to one side. If there is any likelihood of vomiting or breathing becomes difficult, place the casualty in the Recovery Position (see opposite). Keep the patient warm, but not too hot.
- Remain with the patient and give reassurance. This should be as specific as possible — explain what is happening and what treatment is being given.
- Under no circumstance give anything to drink, but lips should be moistened with water, one or two drops of a homeopathic remedy or the Bach Flowers Rescue Remedy. Do *not* give the casualty a cigarette, alcoholic drink or hot water bottle, even if asked for.
- Suggested homeopathic remedies:
Arnica montana: for shock from physical injury and bleeding.
Veratrum album: for a cold sweat on the forehead, heart problems or a hypersensitive nervous system.

SNAKE BITES

If you come across a snake, STOP. DO NOT MOVE. The snake will go away. On no account attempt to run away or chase the snake and do not scream, gesticulate or do anything to alarm the creature. NEVER put out your hand towards the snake or attempt to touch it.

Treatment

- Give the Bach Flowers Rescue Remedy (p. 17) followed by ledum 30 every half hour and hypericum 30 every ten minutes and at decreasing intervals after the first hour.
- Keep the patient still. Unless you know that you can obtain specific anti-venom within a short space of time, the best possible thing to do is to keep the patient absolutely still.
- Bathe the wound in urine or in hypericum lotion, if possible.
- Be particularly careful not to move the affected area.
- Do not apply a tourniquet or attempt to incise the wound.

Call for professional assistance.

SPRAINS

A sprain occurs when a joint — often the ankle or wrist — is wrenched or twisted suddenly and the ligaments and/or tendons around the joint become damaged. A sprain is always very painful and often swells up, and, as it is important to rule out the possibility of a fracture, the joint may have to be X-rayed.

Treatment

- Elevate the injured area and apply a tight, cold compress, preferably with ten drops of tincture of arnica added to a cup of cold, boiled water. Replace the compress every twenty minutes.
- Give homeopathic arnica every ten minutes for the first hour, every twenty minutes for the next hour, every half hour for the next two hours and hourly thereafter for the rest of the day. Continue with rhus toxicodendron every two hours for the following day or two.
- If the bone covering is injured take ruta graveolens for a day or two.
- Between compresses, apply the essential oils of lavender, sage and thyme dissolved in a carrier oil and massaged into the area around the sprain during the first two days.

REFERENCE

USING ACUPRESSURE

Acupoints are tiny points all over the body. Acupressure involves either gentle massage or strong stimulation of them, and will help to promote healing in other areas of the body. Often, the position of the acupoint is very far from the area where there is a problem. This is because all the acupoints relate to the network of channels around the body which are known as 'meridians' — see the section on acupuncture, p. 17.

In each case the points should be massaged for one or two minutes, or slightly longer if there is a great deal of pain. This should be repeated daily while the condition persists. However, women in early pregnancy, people under the influence of drink or drugs, or people who have just had a heavy meal should not be treated through acupressure.

Below is a list of the acupoints referred to elsewhere in the book and illustrated on the following pages, as indicated:

ANMIAN 1 (Ex)	176	SHENMEN (H 7)	169
ANMIAN 2 (Ex)	176	SHISHENCONG (Ex)	178
BAIHUI (Gv 20)	175	SPECIAL (low back pain)	179
DAZHUI (Gv 20)	174	TAICHONG (Li 3)	173
ERMEN (TH 21)	171	TAIYANG (Ex)	176
FENGCHI (GB 20)	171	TIANSHU (St 25)	168
FOOT LINQI (GB 41)	172	TIANTU (Ren 22)	174
HEGU (Co 4)	167	TINGGONG (SI 19)	171
HOUSI (SI 3)	169	TINGHUI (GB 2)	171
LANWEI (Ex)	179	WEIZHONG (Bl 54)	171
LIEQUE (L 7)	166	WENLIU (Co 7)	167
NEIGUAN (P 6)	170	XINGJIAN (Li 2)	172
NEIMA (Ex)	179	YANLINGQUAN (GB 34)	172
QUCHI (Co 11)	167	YAOYANGCHUAN (Gv 3)	174
RENZHONG (Gv 26)	175	YINTANG (Ex)	175
SANYINJIAO (Sp 6)	618	YUNGCHUANG (K 1)	170
SHANGYANG (Co 1)	166	ZHIGOU (TH 6)	170
SHANZHONG (Ren 17)	173	ZHONGWAN (Ren 12)	173
SHAOCHONG (H 9)	169	ZUSANLI (St 36)	168
SHAOSHANG (L 11)	166		

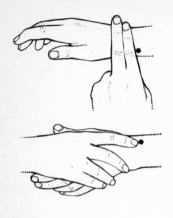

LIEQUE (LUNG 7)

How to find it

On the outer border of the forearm about two fingers' width above the wrist crease immediately above the little bony prominence called the styloid process. It may also be found by crossing the thumbs and first fingers of the two hands as shown. The tip of the index finger will just touch the point.

What to do

Massage the point gently with a fingertip. Repeat regularly for more serious conditions.

Uses

• Headache on the back of the head.
• Asthma, bronchitis and lung disorders.
• Stiff neck.

SHAOSHANG (LUNG 11)

How to find it

At the corner of the nail of the thumb on the outside.

What to do

Massage the point in a circular fashion with a fingertip, or small blunt object, such as the cap of a ballpoint pen.

Uses

• Hysterical attacks.
• Epilepsy and convulsions.
• High fever.
• Cardiac arrest.
• Respiratory arrest.
• Resuscitation of the newborn.
• Acute emergencies.
• Sore throat.
• Numbness of the thumb.
• Acute nasal discharge.

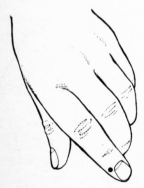

SHANGYANG (COLON 1)

How to find it

At the bottom corner of the nail of the index finger, on the thumb side.

What to do

Massage in a circular fashion with a finger or cap of a ballpoint pen.

Uses

• Toothache.
• Sore throat.
• Numbness of fingers.

HEGU (COLON 4)
How to find it
About one thumb's width in (i.e. towards the wrist) from the edge of the web of skin between the thumb and the index finger.
What to do
Massage in an upward direction, i.e. towards the wrist.
Uses
- This is often known as the aspirin point of acupuncture, since it is the most important point in the body for the control of pain.
- It is related to the front of the head and face: so it is useful for frontal headache, problems of the face and nasal disorders.
- It helps to promote elimination and normalises the function of the large intestine.

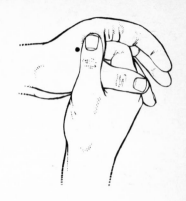

WENLIU (COLON 7)
How to find it
On the back of the lower arm, seven fingers' width from the wrist crease, on a line joining the wrist crease at the base of the thumb and the end of the elbow crease when the arm is flexed to a right angle.
What to do
Massage in a circular fashion, not too gently.
Uses
- Acute sore throat.
- Headache and migraine.
- Aching shoulders.
- Abdominal pain.

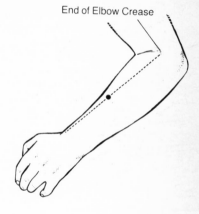

End of Elbow Crease

QUCHI (COLON 11)
How to find it
At the outer end of the elbow crease, when the arm is bent to 90 degrees.
What to do
Massage in an upward direction, towards the top of the arm.
Uses
- This is the best harmonizing point in the body. It is also an immune enhancing point.
- Fever.
- Infections.
- Sprain of the elbow.
- Tennis elbow.
- High blood pressure.
- Skin disorders.
- Pain in the arm.
- Paralysis of the arm.
- Polio.

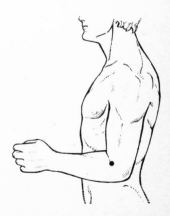

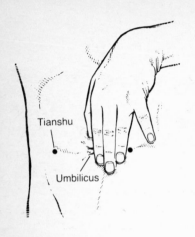

Tianshu

Umbilicus

TIANSHU (STOMACH 25)
How to find it
Three fingers' width either side of the umbilicus (the navel).
What to do
Massage gently with one fingertip, in a circular fashion.
Uses
- Acute and chronic gastro-enteritis.
- Diarrhoea.
- Constipation.
- Intestinal paralysis.
- Abdominal disorders.
- Menstrual disorders.

ZUSANLI (STOMACH 36)
How to find it
Four fingers' width below the lowest point of the knee and one finger's width outwards (i.e. towards the outside of the leg).
What to do
Massage quite firmly in a circular fashion.
Uses
- This is a general toning point. It increases energy and was used by the ancient Chinese before going on a journey.
- It is a homeostatic point for the whole body: i.e. it balances the body.
- It also increases movement of the intestine, and is useful for constipation, diarrhoea, gastritis and digestive problems.
- Helpful for leg and knee pain.
- Also used for dizziness and obesity.

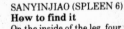

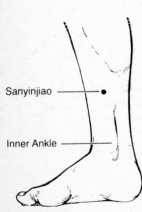

Sanyinjiao

Inner Ankle

SANYINJIAO (SPLEEN 6)
How to find it
On the inside of the leg, four fingers' width above the inner ankle, just behind the leg bone.
What to do
Massage in an upward direction, towards the centre of the body.
Uses
- Menstrual disorders.
- Urine or genital disorders.
- Skin disorders.
- Disorders of the leg.
- Gastro-intestinal problems.
- Muscular disorders.
- Diarrhoea.
- Abdominal distension.
- Leucorrhoea.
- Difficult labour.
- Improves function of the liver, spleen and kidney.

SHENMEN (HEART 7)
How to find it
On the outside wrist crease, just on the
inside of the last tendon at the extreme edge
of the wrist.
What to do
Massage in a circular fashion with the cap of
a ballpoint pen.
Uses
* Insomnia.
* Anxiety and emotional problems.
* Depression.
* Palpitations.
* Mental problems.

SHAOCHONG (HEART 9)
How to find it
At the base of the nail of the little finger, on
the thumb side.
What to do
Massage gently with the cap of a ballpoint
pen.
Uses
* Apoplexy.
* Palpitations.
* Pain in the chest.

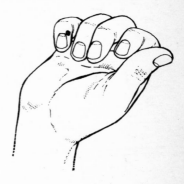

HOUSI (SMALL INTESTINE 3)
How to find it
At the little finger end of the main
widthways crease on the palm. The point is
best located when the fist is lightly
clenched.
What to do
Massage fairly firmly in a circular fashion.
Uses
* Stiff neck.
* Acute low back pain.
* Severe headache at back of head.

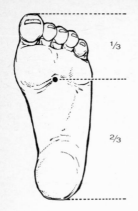

1/3

2/3

YUNGCHUANG (KIDNEY 1)
How to find it
On the sole of the foot, in the centre of the hollow formed when all the toes are bent forward. It lies on a line that divides the second and third toes.
What to do
Massage fairly firmly in a clockwise direction.
Uses
- Fainting, comas and loss of consciousness.
- Apoplexy.
- Useful point generally in emergencies.
- Epilepsy.
- Hysteria.
- Infantile convulsions.
- Nausea and sickness during pregnancy.
- Hysteria.
- Blurred vision.
- Sore throat.
- Dryness of tongue.
- Dizziness.

NEIGUAN (PERICARDIUM 6)
How to find it
Three fingers' width from the mid-point of the wrist crease on the mid-line of the inside of the arm. It is situated between two tendons.
What to do
Massage fairly firmly with a fingertip.
Uses
- Heart disease, including angina.
- Many mental and brain disorders, including epilepsy, insomnia, anxiety and hysteria.
- Nausea and vomiting. Morning sickness.
- Chest pain.
- Hiccups.
- Abdominal discomfort.

ZHIGOU (THREE HEATER 6)
How to find it
On the midline of the back of the arm, four fingers' width from the centre of the wrist crease.
What to do
Massage in a circular fashion with a fingertip.
Uses
- Constipation.
- Hoarseness of voice.
- Aching shoulders.
- Tinnitus.

ERMEN (THREE HEATER 21)
What to do
The ermen point should be massaged towards the centre of the head.
Uses
- Treatment of ear disorders.

TINGGONG (SMALL INTESTINE 19)
What to do
Massage gently with a fingertip in a circular fashion.
Uses
- Treatment of ear disorders.
- Tinnitus.
- Neuralgia.

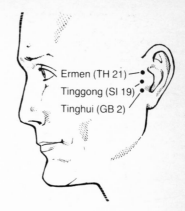

Ermen (TH 21)
Tinggong (SI 19)
Tinghui (GB 2)

TINGHUI (GALL BLADDER 2)
What to do
The tinghui point should be massaged in an upward direction.
Uses
- Treatment of ear disorders.
- Arthritis.
- Facial paralysis.

WEIZHONG (BLADDER 54)
How to find it
At the centre of the crease at the back of the knee.
What to do
Massage fairly firmly in a circular, upwards direction.
Uses
- Back pain.
- Sciatica.
- Paralysis of the leg.
- Problems of the urinogenital system.
- Disorder of the knee.
- Skin problems.

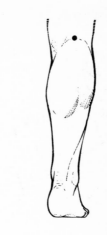

FENGCHI (GALL BLADDER 20)
How to find it
At the back of the neck, slightly above the hair line under the bone of the skull, about two fingers' width on either side of the midline.
What to do
Massage quite firmly in a circular fashion.
Uses
- Headache at the back of the head.
- Common cold.
- Sinusitis.
- Hay fever.
- Influenza.
- Stiff neck and neck pain.

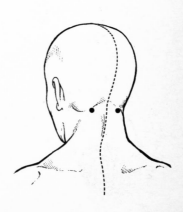

171

YANGLINGQUAN (GALL BLADDER 34)
How to find it
Just below and to the side of the knee cap, in a depression below the head of the fibula (the bone at the side of the leg).
What to do
Massage vigorously in a circular fashion.
Uses
- Knee and leg pains.
- Paralysis of the leg.
- Gall bladder problems.
- Muscular and tendon problems anywhere in the body.
- Mental disorders.
- Epilepsy.
- Headaches.

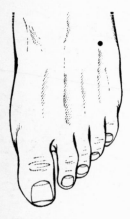

FOOT LINQI (GALL BLADDER 41)
How to find it
Between the fourth and fifth long bones on the foot, near the point where they join together.
What to do
Massage quite gently, towards the top of the foot.
Uses
- Pain in the foot.
- Sore throat.
- Disorders of the breast.
- Ear disorders.
- Frozen shoulder.

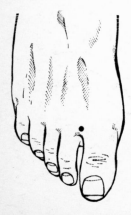

XINGJIAN (LIVER 2)
How to find it
Between the first and second toes, less than one finger's width from the edge of the web of skin.
What to do
Massage gently in a circular fashion.
Uses
- Headache.
- Insomnia.
- Blurred vision.
- Epilepsy.
- Convulsions.
- Retention of urine.
- Heavy menstrual periods.

TAICHONG (LIVER 3)
How to find it
Three fingers' width from the web of skin between the big toe and the second toe.
What to do
Massage gently in a circular fashion.
Uses
- High blood pressure.
- Headache.
- Eye disorders, especially red eyes.
- Sore throat.
- Dizziness.

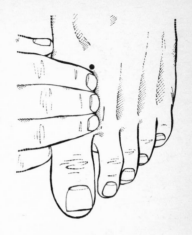

ZHONGWAN (REN 12)
How to find it
In the midline of the abdomen halfway between the navel and the bottom end of the breastbone. It is about four fingers' width above the umbilicus.
What to do
Massage gently, in an upwards direction, towards the head.
Uses
- Flatulence.
- Digestive disorders.
- Constipation.
- Peptic ulcers.
- Abdominal distension.
- Nausea and vomiting.

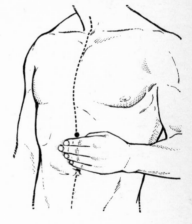

SHANZHONG (REN 17)
How to find it
On the front of the chest midway between the nipples.
What to do
Massage gently in a circular fashion.
Uses
- Bronchial asthma.
- Respiratory problems.
- Disorders of the breast.
- Heart disease.

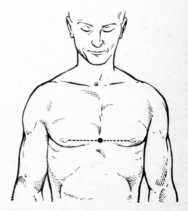

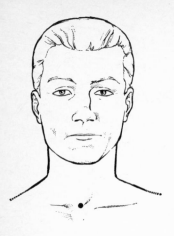

TIANTU (REN 22)
How to find it
At the top of the breast bone. To reach the point, press in towards the throat as far as possible without causing discomfort and then press downwards. It should be possible to get the tip of the finger behind the top of the bone and to press forward.
What to do
Massage gently with one of the smaller fingers.
Uses
- Bronchial asthma.
- Hiccups.
- Pain or difficulty in swallowing.

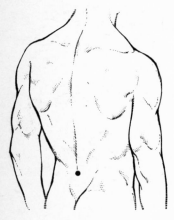

YAOYANGKUAN (GOVERNOR 3)
How to find it
On the back, between the fourth and fifth lumbar vertebrae. It lies at the same level as the upper part of the hip bones.
What to do
Stimulate with circular movements of the inner finger.
Uses
- Low backache.
- Impotence.
- Urino-genital problems.
- Numbness and pain in the legs.
- Muscular weakness or paralysis in the legs.

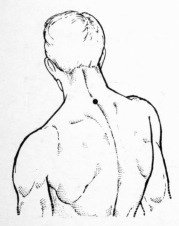

DAZHUI (GOVERNOR 14)
How to find it
At the base of the back of the neck, between the two most prominent vertebrae.
What to do
Massage the point gently with a fingertip.
Uses
- Mental disorders, epilepsy and convulsions in children.
- Headache and migraine.
- Infections.
- Neck disorders and neck injuries.
- Frozen shoulder with loss of power in the arm.
- Lung disorders including bronchial asthma, bronchitis, cough and whooping cough.
- Eczema and skin problems.

BAIHUI (GOVERNOR 20)
How to find it
Draw an imaginary line from the bottom of
the ear lobes to the apex of the ears and
project this over the head. Where it crosses
the midline on the top of the head is the
acupoint.
What to do
Stimulate the point with a fingertip.
Uses
- This is the most powerful tranquillizing
  and sedative point in the body.
- Psychiatric disorders.
- Epilepsy.
- Insomnia.
- Parkinson's disease.
- Impotence.
- Headaches, especially those at the top of
  the head.
- Loss of memory.
- Piles and problems of the anal region.

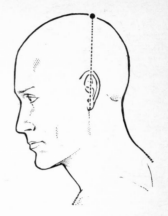

RENZHONG (GOVERNOR 26)
How to find it
On the midline between the nose and the
upper lip, one-third of the way down from
the nose.
What to do
Stimulate the point vigorously with a
fingernail. In emergencies, continue
stimulation until the patient recovers.
Uses
- This acupoint is very useful in acute
  emergencies such as fainting attacks,
  epileptic fits, convulsions, hysterical
  attacks, heat stroke and shock.
- Acute low back pain.
- Facial paralysis.
- Swellings or painful disorders of the
  face.

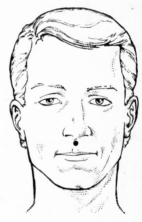

EXTRA POINTS

YINTANG
How to find it
Midway between the inner ends of the
eyebrows, just above the bridge of the nose.
What to do
Massage gently with a fingertip.
Uses
- Headache.
- Migraine.
- Blurred vision.
- Eye problems.
- Runny nose.
- Hormonal problems.

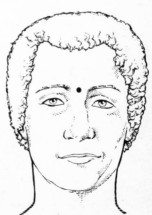

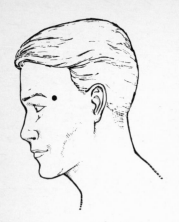

TAIYANG
How to find it
One thumb's breadth behind the eyebrow at the level half way between the outer end of the eyebrow and the corner of the eye. It lies in a dip in the skin.
What to do
Gently massage the point in a circular fashion.
Uses
- Heaache.
- Migraine.
- Eye disease.
- Red eyes.
- Facial paralysis.
- Neuralgia.
- Dizziness.
- Distortion of the mouth.

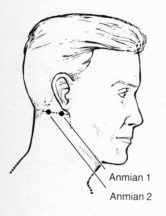

Anmian 1
Anmian 2

ANMIAN 1 AND ANMIAN 2
How to find them
Draw an imaginary line from the edge of the hair line behind the ear to the inner edge of the ear lobe. Divide the line into four. Anmian 1 is one-quarter of the way from the ear lobe, and anmian 2 is three-quarters of the way from the ear to the hairline.
What to do
Massage each or both points with a fingertip.
Uses
- Insomnia.

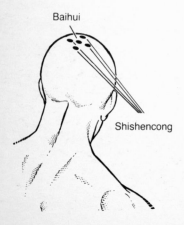

Baihui

Shishencong

SHISHENCONG
How to find them
One thumb's width behind, in front of and to each side of baihui (Governor 20) (see p. 175).
What to do
Massage any of the points very gently with a fingertip. For severe conditions, massage each in turn.
Uses
- Insomnia.
- Anxiety and emotional problems.
- Headache.
- Apoplexy.
- Mental problems.

LANWEI
How to find it
Three fingers' width directly below the point zusanli (Stomach 36) on the knee (see p. 168).
What to do
Stimulate the point with a fingertip or pen cap.
Uses
- The point is often painful when the appendix is inflamed and is therefore useful for the diagnosis, and treatment, of appendicitis.

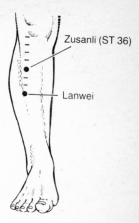

Zusanli (ST 36)

Lanwei

NEIMA
How to find it
On the inner border of the leg bone half way between the inner ankle and the inner border of the knee crease.
What to do
Massge quite gently with a fingertip.
Uses
- For pain relief after lower abdominal, pelvic or perineal surgery.
- For pain control during childbirth.
- For bleeding from the uterus.

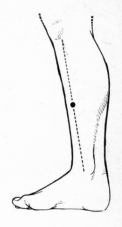

SPECIAL POINTS FOR LOW BACK PAIN
How to find them
Two fingers' width from the 'v' found between the middle finger and the fingers each side of it when the fingers are splayed out.
What to do
Massage with a fingertip in a circular fashion.
Uses
- Pain in the lower back or kidneys.

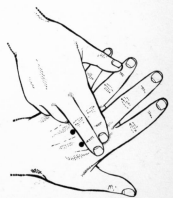

YOGA POSTURES

The benefits of yoga are many and varied. The following postures, as recommended elsewhere in the text, are all beneficial for particular complaints. Yoga is also an excellent way of relaxing and is often recommended as a treatment for those with stress-related problems.

Even if you have never practised yoga before, you will find most of these postures quite straightforward and, with practice, increasingly easy. Spend 10 to 15 minutes each day on the appropriate exercises, repeating them several times, or as often as you can.

Always wear loose, comfortable clothing for the exercises and start by taking a few slow deep breaths. Then relax and take your time over the exercises.

To enjoy the full benefit of yoga, it is advisable for beginners to join a yoga class. There are very many of these, so check with a relevant yoga organization or your local library, advice centre or healthfood shop for details of classes in your area.

ARDHA MATSYENDRASANA (Half twist posture)
This posture is an excellent treatment for all the spinal nerves. It helps to cure constipation and indigestion and is a useful posture for diabetes and kidney problems.
Method
- Start in a sitting position with your legs stretched out in front of you.
- Bend the left knee and bring the heel under your bottom.
- Place your right foot by the side of the left thigh near the knee.
- Bring the left hand round the outside of your right knee and hold the right big toe.
- Take the right hand round the back and grasp the left thigh.
- Look back over your right shoulder and hold for a moment.
- Relax, return to the starting position and repeat on the other side.

VAJRASANA (Ankle posture)
This posture is useful for meditating, it is also helpful for varicose veins and for stiff ankles and knees.

Method

- Sit back on your heels. Keep the knees close to each other, with the spine erect and the head, shoulders and buttocks in a vertical line.
- Ensure that the toes are fully flexed and that the upper surface of the toes is against the floor.
- Rest the palms on the upper part of the thighs or the knees.
- Breathe deeply, with your mouth slightly open.

SUPTA VAJRASANA (Lightening posture)
This posture relieves spinal pain and tones the muscles of the spine. It also exercises the muscles of the feet, knees, abdomen, thorax and neck and improves the blood supply. It also aids digestion, so can be practised after a meal.

Method

- Sit back on your knees as for the Vajrasana posture (top).
- Move your heels slightly to allow you to bend backwards till your head and shoulders touch the ground. As much of the back as possible should be in contact with the ground.
- Clasp your hands loosely behind your back.

BHUJANGASANA (Cobra)
This posture is good for the heart, for reducing abdominal fat and relieving constipation and flatulence. It is also beneficial for the spine. It improves the soft tissue around the spine and tones the muscles, ligaments, tendons, nerves and blood vessels of the spine region. It is also helpful for menstrual problems and PMT.

Method

- Lie face down and place your hands beside your shoulders, facing the front.
- Breathe in as you raise your chest and head, stretching the head backwards. The body from the waist down should remain in contact with the floor and both legs and feet should be held together.
- Breathe slowly and deeply whilst holding the position, then relax onto the floor.

SALABHASANA (Locust posture)

This posture relieves constipation and tones the kidneys. It also improves the muscles of the hips and lower back.

Method

- Lie face down on a blanket keeping the legs together, the chin on the ground and the soles of your feet facing upwards.
- Make a fist with the thumb inside and place your hands under your abdomen.
- Inhale and hold the breath. Raise your legs from the waist and lift your head off the ground. Keep your legs straight. Relax and breathe out.

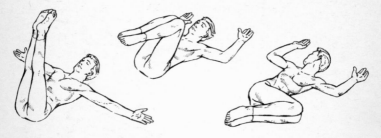

JATHARA PARIVARTANASANA

(Torsion of the abdomen)

This posture tones up the abdominal area, particularly the liver, spleen and pancreas.

Method

- Lie on your back with your arms stretched out at right angles to your body.

- Raise the legs, keeping them straight while breathing out.
- Bend the knees and lower them to the left side whilst turning your head to the right. Pause for half a minute or longer, concentrating on the abdominal area.
- Repeat to the right side.

UDDIYANA BANDHA (Flying contraction)

This posture is very effective in the treatment of constipation, digestive problems and hiccups. It also tones up all the abdominal organs and helps to break down abdominal fat.

Method

- Stand with your legs apart and your hands on your thighs. Bend your head forward with your chin as near to your chest as possible. Take a full breath.
- Exhale completely and, pressing with your hands on your thighs, pull the stomach upwards towards the chest. Repeat this several times while holding your breath.

PAVAN MUKTASANA (Wind releasing posture)

This posture aids digestion and is particularly helpful for flatulence.

Method

- Lie on your back with your arms stretched out. Breathe out.
- Raise the right leg to a 45 degrees angle. Keep the left leg firmly on the ground and breathe in partially.
- Bring the right leg to a perpendicular position and complete the inhalation.
- Bend the right knee and pull it up to

your chest. At the same time lift your head and upper back upwards off the floor. Breathe out.

- Straighten the body and leg again so that toes point towards the sky. Breathe in.
- Bend the knee again and place your chin on top of the knee. Rotate the left leg in an eliptical fashion, first clockwise, then anticlockwise, five times in each direction. Breathe normally.
- Return to the starting position and repeat with your left leg.

DHANARASANA (Bow posture)

This posture improves the condition of the lumbar discs in the spine and stimulates the sexual organs and kidneys. It also relieves constipation and helps avoid the formation of cellulite.

Method

- Lie face down on the floor.
- Bend your knees and grasp your heels.
- Push your legs into the air and raise your chest.
- Hold for about one minute.

VITAMINS AND MINERALS

FOODS RICH IN IRON
Essential for the correct functioning of oxygen in the body and for a healthy pregnancy.

Kelp	Molasses	Pumpkin
Soya beans	Wheat bran	Squash
Lima beans	Dandelion leaves	Red peppers
Green vegetables	Pistachio nuts	Sunflower seeds
Liver	Eggs	Dried apricots
Almonds	Kidneys	Cashew nuts

FOODS RICH IN VITAMIN A
Essential for good eyesight, clear skin, strong nails and to produce essential mucus to line the body cavities.

Yellow fruits	Yellow vegetables	Apricots
Dark green	Cod liver oil	Egg yolks
vegetables	Dandelion	Carrots
Red peppers	Peaches	Prunes
Kale leaves	Mustard	Parsley
Spinach	Turnip greens	Beetroot
Chives	Watercress	Butter

FOODS RICH IN VITAMIN B1 (THIAMINE)
Important for good digestion and the proper functioning of the nerves and brain.

Brewer's yeast	Whole grains	Blackstrap molasses
Wheatgerm	Brown rice	Soya beans
Peanuts	Chickpeas	Sesame seeds
Millet	Egg yolks	Mung beans
Broad beans	Red beans	Lima beans
Cashew nuts	Yeast	Liver

FOODS RICH IN VITAMIN B12 (COBALMIN)
Necessary for red blood cell production, good digestion and a strong nervous system.

Liver	Eggs	Kidneys
Cheese	Wakame (seaweed)	Oily fish

FOODS RICH IN FOLIC ACID
Important for red blood cell production, healthy pregnancy, sound digestion and normal brain functioning.

Brewer's yeast	Liver	Wheatgerm
Kidneys	Nuts	Green vegetables

FOODS RICH IN VITAMIN C
Essential for production of healthy connective tissue, good bone structure, resistance to infection, absorption of iron.

Oranges	Green peppers	Blackcurrants
Tomatoes	Rosehips	Potatoes
Acerola cherries	Sprouting seeds	Peas

FOODS RICH IN VITAMIN B2 (RIBOFLAVIN)
Essential for healthy skin, clear eyes, a strong nervous system and uninterrupted sleep.

Yeast	Chicken	Liver
Apricots	Green vegetables	Tomatoes
Milk	Wheatgerm	Bran
Cheese		

FOODS RICH IN VITAMIN B3 (NIACIN)
Important for good brain and nerve function, a balanced digestion and the proper energy production of food in the body.

Liver	Wheatgerm	Lean meat
Nuts	Fish	Chicken
Brewer's yeast	Eggs	

FOODS RICH IN VITAMIN B6 (PYRODOXINE)
Essential for assimilating proteins in the body, healthy muscular tissue, nerves and skin.

Brewer's yeast	Oats	Wheat bran
Soya flour	Wheatgerm	Bananas
Milk	Peas	

FOODS RICH IN CALCIUM
Needed for healthy bones, nails and teeth.

Green leafy vegetables	Almonds	
Parsley	Dandelion leaves	Sesame seeds
Milk	Cheese	Soya beans
Watercress	Chickpeas	Yoghurt
Olives	Broccoli	Brazil nuts
Wheat bran	Mung beans	Broad beans
	Tuna fish	Sardines

FOODS RICH IN VITAMIN K
Necessary for proper blood formation (controls clotting).

Green vegetables	Honey	Soya beans
Egg yolk	Tomatoes	Wheatgerm

FOODS RICH IN VITAMIN B13 (OROTIC ACID)
Necessary for good circulation. Supplies oxygen to the heart and blood cells. Acts as detoxicant.

Whole grains	Brewer's yeast	Brown rice
Sunflower seeds	Apricot kernels	Liquid whey
Root vegetables		

FOODS RICH IN VITAMIN P (BIOFLAVONOIDS)
Maintains healthy blood capillaries and helps to ward off infections.

Citrus fruits	Grapes	Blackcurrants
Buckwheat	Apricots	Rosehips
Walnuts	Green peppers	

FOODS RICH IN VITAMIN E
Vital for maintaining healthy blood vessels and muscles. Acts as an antioxidant.

Cold pressed oils	Whole grains	Eggs
Wheatgerm	Heart	Molasses
Leafy vegetables	Green leaves	Nuts
	Liver	Kidney

FOODS RICH IN VITAMIN D
Vital for the healthy formation of bones and the release of energy in the body.

Butter	Cod liver oil	Eggs
Oily fish	Milk	

The body also synthesises large amounts of vitamin D through bright sunshine.

FOODS RICH IN ZINC
Zinc is needed for the correction utilization of vitamin A in the body and for proper insulin activity. It encourages the correct development of the skeletal and nervous system in foetuses.

Pumpkin seeds	Sunflower seeds	Mushrooms
Wheat bran	Brewer's yeast	Wheatgerm
Whole grains	Rye	Brown rice
Walnuts	Cheese	Crab
Liver	Kidney	

FOODS RICH IN MAGNESIUM
Needed for the proper utilization of vitamin B6 and for the healthy growth and repair of body cells.

Kelp	Wheat bran	Wheatgerm
Almonds	Cashew nuts	Soya beans
Brazil nuts	Peas	Peanuts
Beans	Apricots	Figs
Brown rice		Dates

ACID FORMING FOODS		ALKALI FORMING FOODS
All meat	Flours	All fruits
Fish	Grains	All vegetables, except onions
Peanuts	Wheatgerm	Coconut
Brazil nuts	Chocolate	Hazelnuts
Onions	Butter	Soya flour
Pistachio nuts	Butter	Honey
Walnuts	Peanut butter	Maple syrup
Yeast	Margarine	Raw sugar
Bread	Cheese	Milk
Cornflakes	Eggs	Yoghurt

LIVER DRAINAGE

The liver is the largest and most important organ in the body and so it is vital to keep it functioning properly.

It processes the products of the digestive system, processes bile to help break down fats, stores the body's vitamin D supplies and converts toxins into neutralized urine.

An unhealthy liver — often caused by excess alcohol or rich food — can lead to cirrhosis of the liver, jaundice, hepatitis and many other dysfunctions of the body.

Liver drainage — the process by which the liver is cleansed, given a chance to rest and start to function properly again — is an essential first step in curing many different conditions. Clear out the bowel first by taking a tbsp of castor oil with orange juice last thing at night. In the morning there should be a good bowel movement which will help prepare the body for liver drainage.

Method

- Fast for two days on fruit juice or vegetable juice and water only, *or*
- Drink at least one pint of raw or fermented beetroot juice or carrot juice over a period of twenty-four hours. Do not drink too much of the juice too soon in the day, to avoid releasing toxins too rapidly.
- Take vitamins A,C,E, B complex and F.
- Do not drink any coffee, tea or alcohol during this period. Drink dandelion 'coffee' instead.
- Drink plenty of bottled water.
- Hot water with honey and lemon or apple cider vinegar and honey may also be taken.
- Take at least one garlic capsule a day, or a clove of garlic in food.

Two days is usually enough for effective liver drainage.

ELIMINATION DIET

The elimination diet is designed to rest the digestive system and promote good health by detoxifying the tissues. It should be followed for one or two days, or as indicated under specific ailments in the A-Z section.

Breakfast	Citrus fruit, especially grapefruit Fresh papaya (if available)
Mid morning	A glass of fresh or fermented carrot or beetroot juice
Lunch	Raw vegetable salad (no pulses should be included) with a dressing of olive oil and cider vinegar if wished. Raw fruit
Afternoon	A glass of fresh or fermented carrot or beetroot juice
Dinner	Steamed vegetables, or fruit or salad as at lunch
Evening	As mid morning.

USEFUL ADDRESSES

ASSOCIATIONS

U.K.

The Association of Natural Medicine
27 Braintree Road
Witham, Essex CM8 2BS
(0376 511069)

Alexander Research Trust
18 Lansdowne Road
London W11 3LL

The British Acupuncture
  Association
34 Alderney Street
London SW1 4EU
(01 834 3353/1012)

The British Chiropractors'
  Association
5 First Avenue
Chelmsford, Essex CM1 1RX
(0245 353078)

Bach Flower Remedies Ltd
Dr. E. Bach Centre
Mount Vernon
Sotwell, Wallingford
Oxon OX10 0PZ

The Active Birth Movement
35 Dartmouth Park Road
London NW5

Intractable Pain Society of Great
  Britain and Ireland
Pain Relief Clinic
Basingstoke District Hospital
Aldermaston Road
Basingstoke, Hants RG24 9NA
(0256 473203)

National Childbirth Trust
9 Queensborough Terrace
London W2 3TB
(01 221 3833)

West London Birth Centre
7 Waldemar Avenue
London W13 9FZ

The British & European Osteopathic
  Association
7 Sidewood Road
London SE9 2EZ

The British Homeopathic
  Association
27a Devonshire Street
London W1N 1RJ
(01 935 2163)

The British Naturopathic &
  Osteopathic Association
6 Netherall Gardens
London NW3
(01 435 7830)

The British Osteopathic Association
8 Boston Place
London NW1
(01 262 1128)

The College of Osteopaths
  Practitioners Association
110 Thorkhill Road
Thames Ditton
Surrey KT7 0UW
(01 398 3308)

The Faculty of Homeopathy
Royal London Homeopathic
  Hospital
Great Ormond Street
London WC1N 3HR
(01 837 3091 ext. 72)

Society of Teachers of the
  Alexander Technique
10 London House
266 Fulham Road
London SW10 9EL

The General Council and Register of
  Osteopaths
1-4 Suffolk Street
London SW1Y 4HG
(01 839 2060)

The National Association of
  Spiritual Healers
Old Manor Farm Studios
Church Street
Sunbury on Thames, Middlesex
(0327 83164)

The National Institute of Medical
  Herbalists
41 Hatherley Road
Winchester, Hampshire SO22 6RR

The Society of Homeopaths
2a Bedford Place
Southampton SO1 2BY
London SW16

The College of Health
18 Victoria Park Square
London E2 9PF

Independent Midwives Association
65 Mount Nod Road
London SW16 2CP

Naturopathic Nurses Association
31 Imperial Avenue
London N16

U.S.A.
Acupuncture Research Institute
Spring Valley Health Center
3880 S. Jones Blvd
Suite 214, Las Vegas
Nevada 89103

American Academy for Acupuncture
& Auricular Medicine
1634 Gull Road
Kalamazoo
Michigan 49001

American Association of
Naturopathic Physicians
P O Box 5086
New Haven, Conn 06525

American Association of
Acupuncture and Oriental
Medicine
50 Maple Place, Manhasset
New York 11030

International Chiropractors
Association
741 Brady Street
Davenport
Iowa 52808

National Center for Homeopathy
Suite 506, 6231 Leesburg Pike
Falls Church, Virginia 22044

New England School of Acupuncture
319 Arlington Street
Waterton, Massachusetts

National Center of Homeopathy
1500 Massachusetts Ave, NW
Suite 41
Washington DC 2005

Australia
Brisbane College of Traditional
Acupuncture
2nd Floor, Century House
316 Adelaide Street
Brisbane 3000, Queensland

Acupuncture Association of Victoria
126 Union Road, Surrey Hills
Victoria 3127

Nonsuch Botanicals Pty Ltd
P.O. Box 68
Mt. Evelyn, Victoria 3796

Median Research
128 Stuart Road, Warradale
South Australia 5046

Acupuncture College of Australia
520 Harris Street
Ultimo, Sydney
New South Wales

Australian Osteopathic Association
551 Hampton Street
Hampton, Victoria 3188

The Australian Homoeopathic
Association
c/o 16A Edward Street
Gordon, New South Wales 2072

International College of Mineral
Therapy
State Bank Building
2nd Floor, 60 Young Street
Victoria

Canada
Canadian Naturopathic Association
Suite no. 306, Mid Part Center
259 Mid Park Way S.E.
Calgary, Alberta T2X1M2
(403 256 0272)

Canadian Osteopathic Association
375 Waterloo Street
London, Ontario N6 B2 R2

189

USEFUL ADDRESSES

Northern American Academy for
  Acupuncture Research
Box 28, Wheatly
Ontario, NOP 2PO

New Zealand
Register of New Zealand Osteopaths
92 Hurstmere Road
Takapuna, Auckland

The New Zealand Homeopathic
  Society
P.O. Box 2939
Auckland

Society of Osteopaths
560 Main Street
Palmerston North

HOMEOPATHIC PHARMACIES

U.K.
Ainsworth's Pharmacy
38 New Cavendish Street
London W1
(01 935 5330)

A Nelson & Co. Ltd
73 Duke Street
London W1
(01 629 3118)

E. Gould & Son Ltd
34 Crowndale Road
London NW1
(01 388 4752)

Hughes' Chemist
High Street, High Wycombe
Bucks
(0494 30138)

Weleda (UK) Ltd
Heanor Road, Ilkeston
Derbyshire DE7 8DR

U.S.A.
Stamps Apothecary
33 Van Buren
Eureka Springs
Arkansas 72632

Standard Homeopathic Company
Box 61067
Los Angeles
California 90061

SOURCES OF HERBS AND ESSENTIAL OILS

U.K.
Aromatic Oil Co
12 Littlegate Street
Oxford OX1 1QT
(0865 42144)

Culpeper Ltd
21 Bruton Street
London W1X 8DS

Life Tree Ltd
P.O. Box 20, Llandrindod Wells
Powys, Wales LD1 6DF
(0597 4656/7)

Phytoproducts
Tidebrook Manor Farm
Wadhurst, Sussex TN5 6PD

Potters Ltd
Leyland Mill Lane
Wigan
Lancashire WN1 2SB

U.S.A.
Indiana Botanic Gardens
P.O. Box 5, Hammond
Indiana 46325

Luyties
Box 8080, St. Louis
Mo 63156

Nature's Herbs
281 Ellis Street
San Francisco, California 94102

No Common Scents
Kings Yard, Yellow Springs
Ohio 45387

Nutridyn
14802 N.E. 31st Circle
Redmond, Wa 98052

A HOLISTIC
FIRST AID BOX

Every home should have a First Aid box, for situations where you do not wish to waste time hunting for an essential item. This list of suggested contents is based on the holistic principles of the book and all the items recommended here are mentioned throughout the text.

HOMEOPATHIC REMEDIES

Arnica montana Ø
Arnica montana 30 or 6x
Calendula officinalis Ø or hypercal Ø
Hypericum perfoliatum Ø or hypercal Ø
Hypercium perfoliatum 30 or 6x
Ledum palustre 30 or 6x
Magnesium phosphoricum 6x
Ferrum phosphoricum 6x
Calcarea fluorica 6x

Cotton wool
Scissors
Eyebath
Small magnet
Tweezers
Several different bandages
Face flannel

Essential oils of lavender, thyme, sage,
     rosemary and clove
Bicarbonate of soda
Small bottle of vinegar
Olbas oil
Calendula ointment
Witch hazel
Vitamin E capsules
Bach Flowers Rescue Remedy

ABOUT THE AUTHOR

Michael Nightingale, DO MD(MA), LicAc, FBAcA, FBEO, is both a practising acupuncturist and an osteopath, and uses a wide range of natural therapies in the treatment of his patients.

He lectures to undergraduates in Britain, and is also visiting professor at the International College of Acupuncture in Sri Lanka.

He has written numerous articles on health subjects and several books, including ACUPUNCTURE in Optima's Alternative Health series.